Shirley Toulson

THE WINTER SOLSTICE

JILL NORMAN & HOBHOUSE

For Roy

Jill Norman & Hobhouse Ltd
90 Great Russell Street, London WC1B 3PY

First published 1981
Copyright © Shirley Toulson 1981

British Library Cataloguing in Publication Data
Toulson, Shirley
   The winter solstice.
   1. Religions
   2. Sun (in religion, folk-lore, etc.)
   3. Great Britain–Religion
   I. Title
   291.2'12   BL438

ISBN 0-906908-25-6

Designed by Wendy Bann
Typeset by Inforum Ltd, Portsmouth, Hants.
Printed and bound in Great Britain by
Mansell Print Ltd,
Witham, Essex

CONTENTS

Acknowledgements *vi*

Introduction *1*

1 Stone Age Sun Markers *7*

2 The Celts: Samhain to Imbolc *18*

3 The Romans: from Saturnalia to Christmas *32*

4 Yuletide: the Gods of the North *43*

5 Fire and Light *55*

6 The Plants of the Solstice *70*

7 The Animals of the Solstice *87*

8 Mummers and Guizers *101*

The Winter Festivals *116*

Index *117*

ACKNOWLEDGEMENTS

The research for this book was mostly done in the Bodleian Library in Oxford, and in the library of the Folk Lore Society, University College, London. I should like to express my appreciation to the staff of both places for the help they gave me in my work. I am also grateful to have been granted access to the library of the American Museum at Bath. In addition I want to thank the librarians in the public libraries at Henley-on-Thames and Wells for the trouble they went to in acquiring the books I needed. The most relevant of these are listed in the references to each chapter.

Many people gave up their time to write to me about, or to talk over, the rites of the winter solstice. I gratefully acknowledge the help I received from them, and would like to mention especially the poet, George Mackay Brown, who gave me valuable information on the folklore of Orkney and Shetland; the writer and folklorist, Ralph Whitlock, to whose books I am much indebted, and who was kind enough to procure the picture of the Dorset Ooser for me; the architect, Alison Smithson, who holds regular exhibitions based on the old traditions of Christmas, and who generously made her catalogues and booklists available to me; Robert Harris of old Father Abraham at Hatherleigh in North Devon, who is an authority on mummers' plays; and Jim Kimmis, who allowed me to share his research on the calendar of pre-Roman festivals in this country.

Finally I want to thank my son, Ian Toulson, who gave up his time and used his computing skills to help me compile the index.

LIST OF ILLUSTRATIONS

Page 8	Newgrange, Co. Meath, Ireland (Irish Tourist Board)
Page 11	Long Meg and her daughters, Cumbria (John Glover)
Page 12	Cornish fogou by Oliver Caldecott
Page 13	The Dorset Cursus (John Boyden)
Page 19	British camp above Whiteleaved Oak by Oliver Caldecott
Page 21	Mistletoe by Mary Jane Toulson
Page 22	Maiden Castle, Dorset (Royal Commission on Historical Monuments)
Page 24	The giant of Cerne Abbas, Dorset (British Tourist Authority)
Page 27	Hazelnuts by Mary Jane Toulson
Page 29	Bridestones Long Barrow, Staffordshire by Oliver Caldecott
Page 37	Sagittarius (Helen Gleadow)
Page 40	St Martin's Church, Canterbury (British Tourist Authority
Page 41	Sul-Minerva figurine (Institute of Archeology, Oxford)
Page 43	Reconstruction of Saxon huts, West Stow by Oliver Caldecott
Page 49	Sutton Hoo helmet (Trustees of the British Museum)
Page 53	Up Helly Aa, Shetland (British Tourist Authority)

Page 58	*Lewes bonfire celebrations, Sussex (British Tourist Authority*
Page 59	*Hatherleigh Fire Festival, Devon (George Tucker)*
Page 60	*North Somerset Pageant (Eric Purchase)*
Page 63	*Christingle Service (Church of England Children's Society)*
Page 63	*Christingle by Mary Jane Toulson*
Page 65	*Hanukkah Festival (Peter Fisher)*
Page 70–85	*Plant illustrations by Mary Jane Toulson*
Page 89	*The Smithfield Cattle Show, Islington (London Illustrated News)*
Page 90	*Dorset Ooser (Ralph Whitlock)*
Page 92	*Kentish hodening horse (Ronald White)*
Page 93	*Häggeby Stone, Uppland, Sweden (Riksantikvarambetet)*
Page 96	*Hunting the Wren, Isle of Man (The Manx Museum)*
Page 97	*Wren by Barclay Wills*
Page 107	*Keynsham mummers (Peter Barnfield)*
Page 107	*Marshfield mummers (Peter Barnfield)*
Page 113	*Abbots Bromley Horn Dance, Staffordshire (Rugeley Times, Staffs.)*

INTRODUCTION

'The Sun is God'
Deathbed saying attributed to the painter, WILLIAM TURNER.

The need to celebrate the return of the longer days, as the seasons turn around at mid-winter, is compulsive. Nowadays no-one can avoid paying attention to Christmas, however much we complain about the commercialisation of what we like to think of as a simple family holiday; and however remote we may feel from the festivals of the Church, which itself has often been a reluctant participant in the ceremonies of the mid-winter holiday. For Christians, Easter must be the most important time of the year, and for centuries it was kept so, but people could not be prevented from celebrating at mid-winter.

The Protestants were especially opposed to any great feast on 25 December; and in the seventeenth century the Puritans were so determined to put an end to the Christmas holiday that, on Wednesday, 22 December 1647, the Canterbury crier went through that city proclaiming that Christmas Day and all other superstitious festivals should be put down and that a market should be kept open on Saturday, 25 December, which was to be treated just like any other day. Five years later, on Christmas Eve, a general order of Parliament decreed 'that no observation shall be had of the five and twentieth day of December, commonly called Christmas Day, nor any solemnity used or exercised in Churches upon that day in respect thereof'.

Yet Christmas survived, and with it all the traditions that embody the pagan ceremonies which surround the solstice, and which still compel our observance, although we are often unaware of their origins. The early Christian fathers were well aware of the pagan rites and made use of them to further their own ends. St Augustine did not try to put a stop to the mid-winter festivals but exhorted the brethren 'not to solemnise the day on account of the sun like the heathen, but rather on account of Him who made the sun'. More practical still, at a time when Christians were liable to persecution, the Greek Father Chrysostom defended the choice of 25 December as the date to celebrate Christ's nativity by reasoning that 'while the heathen were busied with their own profane celebrations, the Christians might perform their holy rites without molestation'.

In holding the feast of Christmas at the time of the winter solstice, and in demanding that people took a holiday at that time, the early Church was acting very wisely. People would have celebrated the season anyway, for it is only in the past three hundred years or so that a 'rational' civilisation has turned its back on both the Christian and the pagan traditions and marked the solstice by custom and habit rather than by an instinctual involvement with the turning seasons. The seventeenth-century antiquarian, John Aubrey, who lived through the years of Puritan domination, saw quite clearly how 'the old tradition-soaked culture' was giving way to 'the new mechanical civilisation', as one present-day commentator on his work has put it.[1] He added that Aubrey saw this change as 'affecting not only tales and fables but also ancient customs and festivals dating from Roman times, which had indeed blended with Roman and Anglican rites'. Confused as he was about the dates and practices of the Druids, I am sure that Aubrey would have agreed that many of the rites the Catholic Church took over were in fact pre-Roman.

This belief that the future of the true life of the Church (as opposed to its administration) is inextricably bound up with an awareness of the pagan festivals has never completely died. In the early years of this century a young woman who wrote under the name of Michael Fairless and whose last book, written while she was dying, was to become popular household reading, declared, 'We can never be too pagan when we are truly Christian, and the old myths are eternal truths, held fast in the Church's net.'[2]

The old myths grew out of the seasonal divisions of the year, and the seasons are reckoned according to the different ways that men have depended on the fluctuations of weather and daylight. One of the reasons that we have lost the true meaning of those myths today is that, in our urban, mechanical civilisation, our dependence on the weather is only brought home to us in extreme conditions such as an unusually prolonged drought or remarkably severe snowfall. We have replaced the calendar by the diary and the long-term planner, arranging our years according to individual business commitments. For our ancestors, the calendar, whether enshrined in myth or ritual, marked out by meticulously calculated stone circles or actually computed and written down for long cycles of years (the Celts based theirs on a nineteen-year run) was of vital importance to the whole community.

The division of the year was governed completely by the way men made use of the seasons. Because of their reliance on the mid-points of winter and summer, on the start of spring which marks the time for planting seeds and the birth of animals, and on early autumn when plants ripen to harvest and young animals are large enough to be hunted, Stone Age hunters and early arable farmers divided the year, as we do, into four seasons.

The people whose lives were more bound up with their livestock, and who were pastoral rather than arable farmers, made a different distinction. For them there were not four seasons but two, winter and summer, dark and light. The flocks and herds were either grazing on the hillsides, or they were in the byres or sheltered valleys, dependent on whatever extra food the stockmen could give them. These people ignored the solstices and equinoxes and concentrated on those times when there is a more definite shift in the climate. For the Celts, therefore, the winter began in early November, when the cattle were brought down from the summer pastures, and it went on until the following May Day when they could go up to the hills again. They did, however, make a festival in early February, when the dark months begin to lighten and the new lambs are born.

The traditions that have fashioned our winter celebrations take all these divisions into account, starting with the Celtic festival of Samhain on 1 November and continuing to Imbolc on 1 February. In Christian terms one can say that they stretch from All Saints' Day to Candlemas.

Naturally the climatic seasons vary according to latitude, and we must expect to find many differences between our nature myths and those of arctic or equatorial regions. As this book concentrates on the winter solstice customs in Britain, I shall draw almost exclusively on those myths that pertain to our own northern and temperate zone. This gives a lot of scope, for our rituals have been fed from both the classical myths of the sunlit Mediterranean and from the harsh, cold, dark countries of Scandinavia. This is not simply because Britain has traded with these regions for millennia, and endured occupation by them at specific periods in her history. We share some of the Mediterranean rituals because up to the time of the Bronze Age many areas of southern England, which never suffered an ice age, were so mild that the climate could be compared to that of some parts of Greece and Italy; whereas the north of Britain, although warmed by the Gulf Stream, still endured the long dark winters of Scandinavia.

All the rites of the winter solstice are attempts to act out the ancient belief that there must be a deliberate death in order that such winters can end, the year turn round and the sun renew its strength. The idea of such a sacrifice is universal, even in near tropical countries. Often the victim is closely identified with the god to whom he is sacrificed. In Mexico, the man who was doomed to die ruled as a king for a full year. Throughout the last twenty days of his reign he was accompanied by four girls who were thought of as goddesses. This protomonarch took the place of Tezcatlipoco (the Sun God in his aspect of darkness), and he was ritually slaughtered at the temple of Quetzalcóatl. Jacquetta Hawkes interpreted it thus: 'It seems that the whole solar year was an enactment of the solar cycle, and the last twenty days perhaps representing the time of the winter solstice, and the four goddesses of the earth trying to hold back the sun. The final sacrifice would then symbolise the sun's escape – and indeed further rites which immediately followed seem to have represented the return of the Day Sun, the resurrection of the year.'[3]

In this country, up to the time of the mid-nineteenth century and the advent of cheap lighting, people depended on the sun and the moon rather than on clocks as a way of measuring time. As Richard Jefferies[4] noted, 'the population dwelling in villages and hamlets, and even in little rural towns, saw indeed the sun by day and the moon by night, and learned the traditions and customs of their forefathers, such as had been handed down for generations.' Behind those customs, often transmuted beyond any easy recognition, there is always some trace of the ritual sacrifice that marked the death and resurrection of the sun god at the time of the winter solstice.

In order to look at these customs more clearly, I have divided this book into two parts. The first consists of a chronological study of the non-Christian rites of winter in this country, from the Neolithic era to the Danish invasions of the ninth and tenth centuries AD. In the second part I have looked at the four major components of those rites, which were all closely linked with man's dependence on and relation to the natural world. Three chapters are devoted to the themes of fire, plants and animals, and one to the role that man gives himself in the rituals. That final chapter deals with the mummers and guizers (men dressed in disguises) who took part in the winter plays and pageants which evolved from the ancient rituals and which show man's need to identify with the changing seasons.

I have added a calendar of the dates of all the major festivals that surround the winter solstice. Here I must point out that these dates, as we know them, are of a fairly recent origin, stemming from 1752 when Britain adopted the Gregorian calendar (and so fell into step with the rest of Europe). In that year, to much public outcry about stolen time, 3 September became 14 September. Many people refused to accept the change, especially as it related to Christmas Day, and insisted that the real Christmas Day (Old Christmas) should be celebrated on 5 January and that Twelfth Night was really 17 January. If any particular regional ceremony is marked according to the old calendar, I have noted that in the text.

There is a further confusion about the time of New Year. January 1st was only adopted at the time that we in Britain accepted the Gregorian calendar. Before that, in order to try and put an end to undesirable customs springing from the orgiastic Roman feasts of the Kalends of January, New Year was celebrated on 2 February, the Christian Candlemas, which is also the Celtic festival of Imbolc. The Celts themselves started their new year at the beginning of November, at the season they knew as Samhain and we call All Hallows. They chose the beginning of winter as the division of one year from the next because they counted time by nights rather than days, years by winters rather than summers. In some areas this tradition continued for centuries. So we shall find that celebrations of the New Year in one form or another occur throughout the winter months. For no matter how hard the Church has tried the ceremonies of the winter solstice cannot be tidied up. They are as organic as the natural events they celebrate, and so have their own disorderly, unquenchable life.

References:
1. RICHARD M. DORSON: *The British Folklorists: A History*, Routledge & Kegan Paul, 1968
2. MICHAEL FAIRLESS: *The Roadmender*, Duckworth, 1902
3. JACQUETTA HAWKES: *Man and the Sun*, Cresset Press, 1961
4. RICHARD JEFFERIES: *Round about a Great Estate*, Smith Elder & Co, 1880; Reissued 1903

1 ♦ STONE AGE SUN MARKERS

In the cave which is called Dark Eye
Behind the sun, looking through him as a window
Is the place.

D.H. LAWRENCE, *The Plumed Serpent*

We know very little about the ceremonies and religious rituals by which the Neolithic and Bronze Age farmers who settled in these islands from Dartmoor to the Orkneys ordered their lives. Only one thing is certain; they were sun-worshippers, who went to immense trouble to mark the journey of their deity through the heavens. For although they left no written record of their beliefs, and although their few scratched drawings on rocky surfaces and the cup and ring marks they made on stone are open to several interpretations, we can tell from the orientation and siting of their sacred buildings how important it was for them to monitor the course of the sun and to capture the moment when it set on the shortest day of the year, or when its first rays were visible the next morning.

A temple has been defined[1] as the meeting of time and place, and it is in that sense that I want to look at those prehistoric sites, which we have every reason to suppose were built for religious purposes. In them the original designers created a space whose object was to reflect the sun's changing relationship to the earth, no phase of which could be more momentous than its apparent death and rebirth in mid-winter. In these 'temples' we too can bridge the gulf of time that separates us from our distant ancestors and realise our common human dependence on the sun.

In Ireland, north of Dublin, on the banks of the River Boyne, is the great tumulus known as Newgrange. Its Gaelic name *An Uamh*

Newgrange, Co. Meath, Ireland

Greine actually means the cave of the sun, and such it is. This shapely mound was once surrounded by a stone circle, which archaeologists believe to have pre-dated Stonehenge by several hundred years. The tumulus itself was built over a large stone chamber with curious and deliberate floor markings. This inner chamber is cruciform in shape, and the first beams of the midwinter sunrise are caught in a stone bowl at the end of one length of this cross, a passage of sixty-two feet. As the sun rises its rays are carefully directed to that spot by a small box-like window above the entrance to this passage.[2]

Scholars still debate whether the ancient Greeks had the circle at Newgrange or our more familiar Stonehenge in mind when they wrote of the Hyperboreans who worshipped Apollo in a spherical temple in the far north. Either place is possible, for there is plenty of evidence of a very early two-way trade between Crete and Britain. As markers of the winter solstice, the great difference between the two temples is that Newgrange marks the solstice sunrise while Stonehenge, in all three phases of its building and re-building, was

8 ♦ The Winter Solstice

designed to catch the last rays of the setting sun on the shortest day.

Stonehenge is still powerful enough to draw tourists in vast numbers, so that the site has had to be protected by firm rulings as to when it may be visited and what parts of it walked over. This means that you can no longer visit the monument during a winter sunset, or stand at its centre at any time. This has only fairly recently been so; a few decades ago it was possible to stand at the centre and see 'the sun set just to the left of the tallest stone behind the altar, that is the remaining upright of the great central trilithon, of which the other stone and the lintel have fallen', and to calculate from that observation that 'if the now fallen central stone of the bluestone horseshoe was of the same height as its neighbours, the setting sun on the day of the winter solstice would have appeared exactly over it, and framed by the stones of the great trilithon'.[3]

That observation, made by Gerald B. Gardiner, suggests that the siting of the bluestones was important for the capture of the dying sun's rays. If that is so, then their re-ordering during the successive phases of the building of the monument was done to enhance that effect. The important feature was always the great arch itself, which Gardiner saw as a frame of death. That opinion was shared by the author of the 1955 guide to Stonehenge, who described the great trilithon as 'the door of the netherworld into which the sun passes at the winter solstice'. Yet for Gardiner the image did not stop there. He believed that the trilithon could also be 'a symbol of the Great Mother, the Goddess from whom the Sun God is reborn', and he imagined that 'the appearance of the red disc of the setting sun glowing between the mighty stones of the trilithon through the gathering winter dusk, would symbolise to these ancient people not only death but the promise of rebirth, alike perhaps for men as for the sun, from the womb of the Great Mother'.

At both Newgrange and Stonehenge the important thing is the way the sun's rays are trapped within a clearly defined space. At other Bronze Age sites, the focus is changed to a point external to the 'temple'. In the case of the stone circles, that external marker is directly aligned either to the centre or to a stone which is in some way carefully distinguished from the others. The markers may be 'outriders', standing stones deliberately erected outside but in direct relation to the circle; or some natural but strikingly formed object in the landscape.

The circle of Eyam Moor in Derbyshire is modest enough in itself. Its grandeur comes from the wide moors, hills and curiously shaped gritstone rockstacks that surround it. Across the valley to the east, just below the rugged edge to the west of Sheffield, is a remarkable natural stack, locally known as Mother's Cap. From the circle the mid-winter sun appears to rise immediately behind it. John Barnatt,[4] who has worked out a detailed analysis of that alignment, believes that it is quite likely that Bronze Age men lit fires behind the rock at dawn on mid-winter day in order to enhance the effect of the sunrise, or even perhaps to substitute for it, should the dawn be heavily overcast. Priests have been known to resort to such theatrical effects when the miraculous fails to occur. Possibly something similar happened in the centre of those stone circles on Dartmoor, in which archaeologists have found evidence of fire but none of cremation or sacrificial burnt offerings.

Yet fire, either external to the circle or in the centre of it, cannot be depended on to give a directed beam of light in the way the sun's rays can, for flames are affected by the vagaries of the wind and are bound to flicker. A sunbeam can actually be caught in a particular place, as it is at Newgrange and Stonehenge, furthermore it can trace a beam of light along the ground. The painter John A. Glover[5] has observed that at the Swinside circle (locally known as Sunken Kirk) near Millom in Cumbria, the winter sunrise forms a path of light through the four entrance stones to the circle. This happens on 13 January, about a month after the solstice; but the alignment is so exact that Glover rules out the possibility that the effect could be due to chance.

He is confirmed in this opinion by his observations of a mid-winter sunset alignment at another Cumbrian circle and its outriders, namely Long Meg and her daughters. In that case it is not the passage of light but of shadow that marks the sun's course. It is an effect that can most easily be seen in snow. Glover writes that the shadow, 'links Long Meg to her nearest daughters and then spills over these to reach right across this very large circle to touch the stones on the other side'.

An even more elaborate device for marking the solstice sunset is to be found ten and a half miles north of Lochgilphead on the west coast of Scotland (NM 830050). This site is marked by a cairn and a man-made terrace on the hillside. Both these structures have been

Long Meg and her daughters, Cumbria

most carefully oriented. By focusing past the cairn, the observer on the platform can see the mid-winter sun setting along the slopes of Bein Shiantaidh, one of the Paps of Jura, which lie twenty-eight miles to the west.[6]

I should like to consider the relics of two other types of monument. Their origins are still obscure, but I believe that they once formed part of the winter solstice observations. They are the underground passages in Cornwall, known as 'fogous', and the parallel earthworks of the Dorset Cursus.

The fogous, which are peculiar to Cornwall, and whose closest resemblance among ancient monuments is to the *souterrains* of Brittany, are short underground passages, lined with granite slabs. They contain no evidence of any burial; and the claim that they were grain storage pits, which some archaeologists have put forward, has never been substantiated. Their dating is also uncertain; for although they are believed to belong in the main to the Iron Age, many fogous incorporate earlier underground structures.

That is true of one of the best preserved and the most easily accessible of the fogous. It stands in the midst of the Iron Age village of Carn Euny (now in the care of the Department of the Environment) which lies between Penzance and Land's End. This tunnel is linked to a circular chamber dating from the Bronze Age, which

Stone Age Sun Markers ♦ 11

could well have been sited in relation to either the midwinter sunrise or sunset, although no-one as far as I am aware has done the delicate calculations that would be needed to prove if that was the case. It is a tempting hypothesis to work on however, for the rays of the rising sun could be directed into it from the tunnel which links it to the fogou to the east; while those of the setting sun might reach it from the west, where a further trench was discovered during excavations on the site in 1969.

The purpose of that trench is still unknown. It could simply have been used during the construction of the chamber, as a way for the builders to remove the rubble and get out themselves after they had roofed the chamber. On the other hand it could have been the entrance for the priest, who officiated at the morning or evening solstice rituals, if such took place here.

The possibility of a priest's entrance is suggested by another beautifully preserved fogou near Larmorna. This one stands in the grounds of a private house, beside the earthwork of an Iron Age hill

a fogou, Carn Euny, Cornwall

The Dorset Cursus

fort. Here again a creep passage leads from the fogou to a chamber lying to the west of it. In this case the other enclosure is a narrow rectangle which ends in an inexplicable false doorway facing south. Again it is tempting to speculate that this was once a priest's entrance, and that he came into the chamber as the light from the east struck its western wall, which stands opposite the entrance from the fogou. As in our own cathedrals and churches, the people advance towards the sanctuary from a doorway opposite the altar, while the priest approaches from the side. Only the discovery of an aperture like the one at Newgrange could prove conclusively that the chambers attached to the fogous were used for solstice rituals. At present there is no evidence either way to show if any of the spaces in the ruined structures were specially designed to allow light to penetrate at special times of the year.

We are on surer ground with the Dorset Cursus, which is thought to have been a processional way. It is marked out by parallel earthworks which stretch for six miles, and which are clearly visible in aerial surveys. From the ground it is not so clear but it runs along the south side of the A 354 between Cashmoor and Woodyates.

Stone Age Sun Markers ♦ 13

The earthworks marking this cursus were built around 2500 BC and were connected with some religious ritual in which they played an important part. Several long barrows have been incorporated into the earthworks or enclosed between them. One of the most remarkable of these, a giant eleven feet high, seventy feet wide and 165 feet long, lies across the south-west of the cursus on Gussage Hill. This marks the place where, for anyone approaching from the east along the processional way, the solstice sun sets. We must remember that the chalk of which both earthworks and barrows were constructed was left uncovered, so that they would gleam like shining stones for miles around.

The Dorset Cursus is the longest but by no means the only Neolithic or Bronze Age processional way in Britain. There are the stone rows of Dartmoor, one of which stretches for over a mile, and which also incorporate barrows and cists; there is the very short route (two hundred yards or so) between the parallel earthworks by the river at Dorchester-on-Thames; and many more lead from stone circles, of which the Avebury avenue is the most impressive.

We can only speculate about the form the winter solstice ceremonies took as they were performed in the Neolithic underground chambers, the Bronze Age stone circles and the various processional ways. Some clues, however, come from two groups of people who are more accessible to us than our own remote ancestors. These are the North American Indians and the witches who were brought to trial in seventeenth-century England. The former, who share our latitude and our seasons if not our climate, still wisely embody many aspects of the stone-age culture on which civilisation is universally based. The devil worship to which the latter confessed, marked them out, as Margaret Murray has convincingly argued, as the guardians of the Bronze Age beliefs which the Celtic Druids displaced.

The different tribes of North American Indians vary as much in their ceremonial rituals as they do in their practical ways of daily life. The one thing they all have in common is that these rituals are based on the worship of the sun. Two aspects of this are worth considering: the sacred underground, circular 'kivas' of the Anasazi and the Navajo of Arizona and New Mexico; and the sun dance of the Plains Indians of Wyoming.

The kiva is the ceremonial meeting place for the initiated men in an Indian *pueblo* or settled township. The ones in the ruins of such settlements in the south-western states of America date from around 650 AD (for the great kiva at Pueblo Bonito in Chaco Canyon) to 1300 AD (for the Anasazi group in North West Arizona). The kivas of Mesa Verde at the southern tip of Colorado date from around 1000 AD.

No matter whether these kivas serve a group of dwellings (the two-hundred-room settlement of Cliff Palace at Mesa Verde has twenty-three small kivas) or mark the central meeting place for the whole community (like the reconstructed Great Kiva of the confusingly named Aztec ruins on the borders of New Mexico and Colorado), they are all built on the same basic pattern. They are all entered from above, and their most holy places are marked on the floor. These are the fire pit and the 'sipapu', a small hole in the ground symbolising the crack in the earth's surface through which mankind was supposed to have emerged at the beginning of time. The smoke from the fire could only escape through the entrance in the roof of the kiva, so that the witchdoctor or shaman descended to perform the ceremony through a cloud of smoke. In Chapter 4 I shall show that this bears out our own tradition that Father Christmas makes his appearance down the chimney.

Inside the kiva the rituals were watched by the initiated who sat on a masonry bench incorporated into the inner circumference of the wall, which was also used for the storage and display of sacred objects. Kivas are still used by some North American Indian tribes for rituals designed to promote the health and well-being of the people, and to herald the re-birth of the winter sun.

Like the chambers at Newgrange and the Cornish fogous, they appear to have been designed to capture the rays of the winter sun in the earth; and like our stone circles they were carefully calibrated as calendars, being aligned on marks in the landscape external to themselves, or incorporating slots in the upper edges of their outer walls which monitored the rising and setting of the sun and moon throughout the year.

Although we know very little of the secret sacred rites of the kivas, it is certain that they were performed by masked shaman priests, dressed in the skins of animals and attended by warriors whose feathered head-dresses symbolised the rays of the triumphant sun. At the sacred circle of Medicine Wheel in the Bighorn mountains of Wyoming, men similarly attired took part in the great midsummer Sun Dance of the Plains Indians, which was regularly performed up to the nineteenth century. That open-air ceremony could be watched by all the people of the tribe, although they were kept apart from the main participants. In Britain many of the stone circles are surrounded by earthworks (whose inner ditch shows clearly that they were never intended for defence) from which the people could watch the sacred rites performed by the initiates. The clearest example of this is the wide bank surrounding the three circles at Avebury.

I have taken the examples of a midsummer rite of the North American Indians because it shows most clearly the sort of circular ring dances which I think were performed in our own stone circles at both the winter and the summer solstices. From a few European cave drawings going back to palaeolithic times, we know that masked men dressed in animal skins were also the leading figures in such rituals here. I shall have more to say about them in the last chapter, which deals with the Christmas mummers.

Margaret Murray claims that the masked men of the cave drawings survived as the gods of the witches and became leading figures in each coven, whose members worshipped them as master. Furthermore she concluded that these worshippers were themselves direct descendants of the Neolithic and Bronze Age people who participated in the solstice rites at the stone circles. From them we inherit the ring dances, which could be taken so fast that they induced dizziness and hallucinations. Many stone circles in Britain are said to be maidens petrified for dancing on the sabbath. This, as Ruth St Leger Gordon[8] points out, has nothing to do with Sunday observance but refers to the witches' sabbat, a word derived from the French *s'ébattre*, to frolic.

We also have a tradition of dances in which the participants join hands to form a line, and I believe that something like this must have taken place along the Dorset Cursus and the other processional ways. The 'furry' dances of England (such as the famous one at Helston in Cornwall) take their name from 'fairy'. Margaret Murray has shown conclusively that these fairies, who danced along the processional ways, were not the daintily named creatures whom she discovered in Shakespeare's *Midsummer Night's Dream*, but Bronze Age people, dwelling in caves or in circular huts by their barrows on the open moorland, who were both feared and enslaved by the larger, stronger and more technically able Celts, whose own winter ceremonies are the subject of the next chapter.

References:
1. KEITH CRITCHLOW: *Time Stands Still*, Gordon Fraser, 1979
2. MARTIN BRENNAN, *The Boyne Valley Vision*, Dolmen Press, 1980
3. GERALD B. GARDINER: *The Meaning of Witchcraft*, Aquarian Press, 1959
4. JOHN BARNATT: *Stone Circles of the Peak*, Turnstone Books, 1978
5. JOHN A. GLOVER. Article in *The Ley Hunter* Number 87
6. For a fuller description *see* EVAN HADINGHAM: *Circles and Standing Stones*, Heinemann, 1975; PETER LANCASTER BROWN: *Megaliths and Masterminds*, Hale, 1979
7. MARGARET A. MURRAY: *The God of the Witches*, Sampson Low, Marston & Co., 1931
8. RUTH E. ST LEGER GORDON: *The Witchcraft and Folklore of Dartmoor*, Robert Hale, 1965

2 ♦ THE CELTS: SAMHAIN TO IMBOLC

I reverance not the voice of birds
Nor sneezing, nor any charm in the wide world,
My Druid is Christ the Son of God.

Hymn of St Columba

In the seventh century AD, St Columba is said to have come across a Druid called Broichan in the wild country around Inverness.[1] His hymn could have resulted from that encounter. In any case, the tradition that such a meeting took place is strong enough to make us certain that, whether as priests or sorcerers, the Druids existed for many years alongside the Christian saints. In this chapter, which looks at the winter festivals they presided over, I also hope to show how they kept alive many of the religious customs of the earlier inhabitants of these islands, whom they both feared and enslaved.

When the Celts came to Britain during the first century BC their superior physical strength and the cunning they had in the use of iron made it possible for them to take over the best land and reduce many of the people to slavery. They did this to such an extent that the Roman geographer, Strabo, noted that slaves were among the chief exports of the ancient Britons. Those who were not enslaved were driven to taking refuge in remote places, living beside the burial mounds of even earlier races. They came to exercise a strange power over their conquerors; for the Bronze Age people, whose winter solstice rites were discussed in the last chapter, took on the role of supernatural creatures in the eyes of their Celtic masters.

In the early years of this century a traveller[2] among the Celts of Britain, France and Ireland was told of fairy paths, which were said to be the routes of seasonal processions; and although I have not come across any record of the Dorset Cursus being known as a fairy path it is reasonable to suppose that the Celts did think of it in that way. We do know, however, that the Celts of Dorset and generally throughout Britain worshipped a horned god, as had the Bronze Age people before them. Cernunnos, 'The Horned One', his head surmounted by a stag's antlers, wearing the sacred torc and accompanied by a horned serpent, was the central figure of many Celtic rites.[3]

The actual solstice was not the most important of the Celtic winter festivals although they were clearly aware of it. A Victorian antiquarian[4] let his fancy run wild when he invited his readers to imagine 'that it is the winter solstice, and that the denizens of the British camp and the British town on the Herefordshire Beacon have received the intelligence that, in the valley of the Whiteleaved Oak, a favourite resort of their moral teachers, because of its seclusion, the heaven-sent mistletoe has been discovered growing upon the monarch of the glades, the best-beloved among trees of their great divinity, Tutanes or Haal. Perhaps they have already paid their midday devotions to the great Source of Light; mayhap the moon, to which they will bow in adoration at midnight, has glided within their ken; it may even be the first day of the new moon and therefore a festival; but, be the circumstances what they may, the news will send a thrill of joy through the whole assembly.'

Romantic and far-fetched as that is, it does make three points about the religous practices of the Celts – the priesthood, the sacred places and the Celtic divinities – which must be considered before

British camp above Whiteleaved Oak

The Celts: Samhain to Imbolc ♦ 19

we can hope to make sense of their two great feasts, Samhain and Imbolc which marked the beginning and end of winter. But it is quite misleading to think of the Druids as 'moral teachers' in any sense in which that phrase could be understood today. They were both much more and much less than that. For they were priests, capable of interceding with the gods on behalf of men, and lawmakers concerned with tribal justice; but they had not the sort of ethical responsibility between people which we think of as arising from moral teaching.

The reason we know so little about the Druids and the rituals they presided over is easily explained. Although the Celts were literate, and used Greek for trading purposes, they never committed the secrets of their religion to the written word. The only records we have come from the pens of their enemies, Caesar and other Latin writers, whose interests lay in presenting the Druids as cruel, wild leaders of a barbaric race. In one of his less prejudiced accounts in *De Bello Gallico*, Caesar informs his readers of the long training a would-be Druid had to undergo. He believed that the Druid colleges were first founded in Britain, and that the best students from Gaul still crossed the Channel to attend them. Although there are no accounts of women Druids in Britain, they appear to have existed in Gaul. Vopiscus refers to the powers of prophecy possessed by a Druidess he encountered there.[5]

A few other reliable facts emerge for anyone patient enough to sift through all the prejudiced evidence.[6] The religion of the Celts appears to have had much in common with that of the Hindus, which, as both peoples originate from the same Indo-European race, is not surprising. Like the Hindus, the Celts firmly believed in reincarnation, and they drew their priesthood from young men of the aristocracy, who were thought to have earned their noble birth by merit in past lives.

There are several references in Irish mythology to leading Druids who were supposed to be sorcerers and to have the powers normally associated with a shaman. Anne Ross[7] cites the Irish story of *The Siege of Druim Damhghaire*, which describes a Druid being prepared for a religious ceremony: 'Mog Ruith's skin of the hornless, dun-coloured bull was brought to him then, and his speckled bird-dress with its winged flying, and his druidic gear besides; And he rose up, in company with the fire, into the air and the heavens.'

We know from Pliny that the Celts regarded the mistletoe as a sacred plant possessed of healing properties. This is dealt with more fully in Chapter 6 which is devoted to the plants of the solstice. The widespread but erroneous belief that the Druidic rites took place only in the open air and were almost always celebrated in oak groves also comes from Pliny, who in an account almost as romantic as that of our nineteenth-century historian describes how the mistletoe was cut. According to this, the officiating Druid, dressed in a white robe and carrying a golden sickle, climbed a tree to cut the sacred plant. It was then caught in a white cloak which the other participants in the ritual had spread beneath the tree.

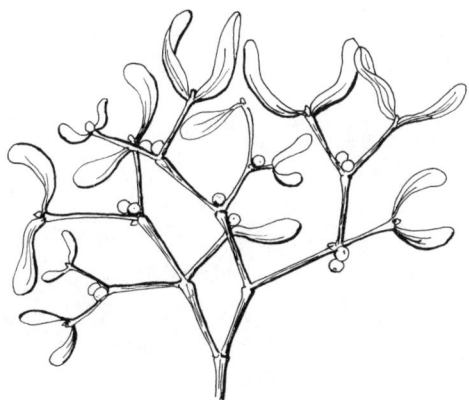

Mistletoe

There must be some truth in that description. The word *druid* is said to originate from the Celtic word for oak, and the sanctity of the combination of that tree with the magical parasite is understandable. Mistletoe is seen commonly enough in apple orchards and growing on lesser trees, but only rarely does it lodge on the boughs of a fully grown oak. Certainly it is reasonable to believe that the Druids had shrines in oak groves, and it is possible to locate some of them, including Whiteleaved Oak itself, which stands at the southern tip of the Malverns. Another is thought to have been at Stonedown Lane to the north of Glastonbury Tor. The oaks that grew there, and which were cut down in 1906, were reported to be of an immense age. Other places are identified as having once possessed Druidic groves because they incorporate some version of the Latin word *nemus*, a grove, into their names. Two such are Vernemeton on the borders of Lincoln and Leicestershire and Bishopsnympton on Exmoor.

Yet archaeological evidence shows that the Celts also used constructed temples, and that these buildings, mostly rectangular structures, were later incorporated into Roman shrines. Some of these, such as the one on the banks of the River Ock (a tributary of the Thames) at Frilford, were based on even earlier religious sites and contained pits full of the remains of sacrificial offerings. These caused the archaeologist D.W. Harding[8] to speculate about a

Aerial view of Maiden Castle, Dorset

22 ♦ **The Winter Solstice**

'religious stability in which cult practices could have survived from remote antiquity into the proto-historic period'. Of Frilford itself he wrote that it 'preserves the form of a religious monument which was current and unique in Britain in the late Neolithic period'. Further Celtic temples, like that dedicated to Nodens (identified with the deified Irish hero Nuadu) at Lydney in Gloucestershire, were not to come into their full glory until the Romans embellished them. Further rectangular Celtic shrines are at Maiden Castle in Dorset and beneath the tarmac of Heathrow airport.

Two temples have a particular bearing on the Celtic winter festivals. They are the rectangular enclosure on the Hill of Tara in Ireland and the grassed rectangle at Kirkstead in Cumbria. The first is popularly known as the Banqueting Hall, and recalls the feasting that was always an integral part of Celtic ritual. The other, in the valley of Loweswater by Kirkhead, has a smaller enclosure within its south-west corner. This is oriented west to east. There is no trace of a wall on the east side, and it has been suggested that this space was deliberately left open so that the priest could stand there to hail the sunrise.

The sun god whom the people of Kirkstead worshipped stood beyond and above the Celtic tribal deities who were honoured at the local shrines. He was Dagda, the good God, the all-father, representing the generating power of heat and light, who fertilised the earth symbolised by the great mother, Anu or Brigit. She has the power to nurture gods as well as men. These lesser gods sometimes presided over particular functions, but in the main they were assigned to places, woods, streams and wells.

The name of Dagda lives on in Irish mythology. In Britain he is thought to be represented by the chalk figure of the Cerne Abbas giant in Dorset, whose cloak, the insignia of Hercules, may have been a Roman addition. In the Christian era, Anu becomes Ann, the mother of the Virgin Mary; and Brigit was canonised as the midwife and wet nurse attending the birth of Christ.

These gods and their progeny demanded human sacrifice. Although there is no evidence to show that it was practised on the scale that Caesar described, there is no denying the fact that the Celts believed their gods required to be propiated with a human life at the great seasonal festivals. The victims whose remains have been discovered in recent years died in various ways, for it was thought

The giant of Cerne Abbas, Dorset

that different gods demanded different forms of sacrifice. So those that were burnt to death died on the altars of Tarinus, the god of Thunder; those who were drowned died to appease Teutates, an equivalent of the Roman Mars; and those who were strangled (like the people found beneath the peat bogs of Ireland and Denmark) are believed to have died to placate the horse goddess, Esus or Epona. Her rites, as we shall see later, seem to have been very similar to the winter solstice rituals of the Norse Odin. Epona was envisaged as a white horse who drew the chariot of the sun.

These three gods have virtually disappeared from our traditions but some of the other Celtic deities have been strangely preserved by the Church. Ann and Brigit have been kept alive by Christian adoption; while the cloven-hoofed Cernunnos has taken on the role of the devil. A direct descendant of the Bronze Age shaman who dressed in animal skins, he appears in varying disguises in traditional winter festivals up to the present day.

The Celts, who were mainly a pastoral people and whose young men spent their summer months with cattle at their upland grazing, kept their main festivals at the beginning and close of winter. As they reckoned time by nights rather than by days, winters rather than summers, Samhain, the start of the cold, dark weeks marked their New Year. This was the time when the cattle were brought to shelter in the byres of the valleys. It fell at the beginning of the month we know as November, and is associated with our traditional observance of All Hallows Eve on 31 October.

Some of the sacrifices that were practised at this season were of a purely practical nature. Many of the animals could not be fed over winter, and so it was wiser to slaughter them for their hides and flesh while they were still in good condition from the summer's grazing. The Celts gave a ceremonial form to this culling, as did the early Neolithic farmers thousands of years before them. In the shallow trenches of the causewayed camp of Windmill Hill near Avebury, piles of carefully arranged animal bones have been found. Scholars conclude that they belonged to the beasts which were slaughtered at the beginning of winter, and which were consumed at some ceremonial gathering of the tribe.

The idea of sacrifice at the start of winter, or immediately after the harvest, is also part of an arable economy. The Celts, who tended fields even though they counted their wealth in cattle, were well aware of the need to prepare for the following year's harvest. According to Irish myth, the fearful one-armed, one-legged Fomoire threatened the whole land with destruction if he did not receive his annual due of one-third of the corn the people produced. This had a practical application; it is generally estimated that in primitive agriculture a third of the harvest must be 'sacrificed' as seed corn.

These practical sacrifices were linked to the human sacrifices the ceremonies demanded. Originally the old king or leader of the tribe gave his life with its failing powers in order that a younger, stronger man could provide for the people. Later another member of the tribe, or even one of its slaves, was chosen as a substitute victim. His selection is supposed to have been made by an unusual system of drawing lots. A feast of oatcakes was held, everyone taking a piece from a large ceremonial dish. In a manner somewhat reminiscent of the story of King Alfred and the burnt cakes, the man who found himself holding a deliberately charred morsel was the victim. It seems to have been a great honour to be chosen to die for the people; and it has been argued that the peaceful, almost happy face of one of the strangled men found in a Danish bog indicates that the victims went gladly to their deaths. In later years an animal, or even some sort of effigy, was substituted for the human sacrifice of Samhain. That custom continues on Guy Fawkes night.

These sacrifices, whether practical or ceremonial, actual or symbolic, all helped to make Samhain a festival of death. This was enhanced by the Celtic belief that any time of change, such as the shift from the months of light to the months of darkness, destroyed the barriers between the living and the dead and between the natural and the supernatural. In the general chaos that ensued, men had to walk warily. The dead were around at this time and, like all of us, the Celts had ambivalent feelings about their return. On the one hand they were terrified of encountering the ghosts of the people they had known in life, and would never look round if they heard footsteps behind them on November Eve for fear of what they might see. To guard against being recognised by a ghost they blackened their faces or wore strange masks to conceal their identity. At the same time, they made as sure as they could that the returning dead should feel welcome. Custom demanded that food should be set out and a good fire made up before the family went to bed on All Hallows Eve. Then, as the door had been left unbolted, the ghosts could come and find shelter for the night.

In some places the fairies as well as the gods and the dead had to be propitiated at this time. These supernatural creatures, who were supposed to live among the Bronze Age barrows and Neolithic tombs, were aroused by this season which eroded all safe distinctions. According to some legends the fairies were so restless at this time that they often moved about the countryside from one abode to another, and those who encountered them while they were changing house could expect misfortune. It was thought unlucky for a place to lose its fairies, and at Newgrange the fairy folk who lived by the great Neolithic barrow were propitiated with the gift of hazel nuts. On the Isle of Man in recent centuries, the left-overs from the family's All Hallows supper were tidily arranged on the table with a jug of fresh water for the fairies. Sometimes the food consumed by the people at a ceremonial gathering was supposed to be shared with beings from another world. This happens at Knutsford in Cheshire where 'soul' cakes are still eaten at All Hallows at a feast lit by candles, whose flames are said to guide the spirits of the dead back to their earthly homes.

Finally, because this season was felt to be such a threatening one for mankind, it was essential that the people should at least be at peace with one another. So at Samhain it was the custom to try and patch up feuds in the same way as we attempt to observe Christmas as a season of goodwill.

The three aspects of Samhain are still kept alive at the beginning of winter. We remember the dead on 2 November, All Souls' Day; recognise the powers of the supernatural on 31 October, when the witches traditionally ride abroad; and keep Armistice Day around 11 November. As for All Saints' Day on 1 November, it was instituted by the Church to channel the pagan observance of Samhain into a Christian mould. As so many of the Celtic gods lived on as Christian saints, this gave the people a sense of protection against the terrors of the time.

Frightened as they were of the ghosts and witches of Samhain, Celtic people used the fearful disruptions of the season as an opportunity to cast omens for the coming year. Above all they wanted to know if they were going to survive the next twelve months; and which of their neighbours were likely to die. The most widely practised form of divination, and one that was kept up at least until the eighteenth century, made use of fire and stone. On the eve of Samhain, every member of the tribe or family group threw an individually marked stone into the embers of the fire. Then 'on the following morning the stones are searched for in the fire, and if any be missing, they betide ill for those that threw them in'.[9] Sometimes hazel nuts were used in a similar way. A nut that burned brightly when thrown into the fire heralded good luck; one that charred and crackled signified disaster and death.[10]

The next nodal point in the Celtic calendar came at the start of February. This was the feast of Imbolc, which marked the beginning of the lambing season. We know far less about the rituals that

Hazelnuts

attended this festival of light than we do about the dark customs of Samhain. Most of its ceremonies have been deliberately and carefully erased by the Church, which instituted the feast of Candlemas at this time. Yet there is some evidence to prove that a February feast was observed even before the Celts gave it a place in their calendar. At least one Bronze Age stone circle, that of Castlerigg in Cumbria, has an alignment on the Candlemas sunrise too precise to be a matter of chance. Another Candlemas alignment was observed by Sir Norman Lockyer at the standing stones known as the Pipers near Land's End.

For the Celts, Imbolc was a season dedicated to Dagda's daughter, the great triple goddess, Brigit, Bridget or Bride, whose name comes from the Sanskrit *Brahti*, the exalted one. At this time of year she is celebrated as the spirit of youth and fertility who is once more abroad in the land. In Scotland they pictured it as the season when Bera, the goddess of winter, who lived on the summit of Ben Nevis and whose silver hammer turned the world to ice released Bride, who had been her prisoner during the winter months.

As a goddess, Bridget was Christianised into a saint who was said to be the foster-mother of Christ in a legend which tells how she acted as midwife and wet nurse at his birth. As St Bridget she has been called the Virgin Mary of the Celts, and although she is based on no known historical figure, her popularity has never waned. At one time The Isle of Man had no less than seven Christian cells named after her as well as a nunnery and a parish church. On that island it was the custom on Candlemas Eve to gather rushes and stand with them at the entrance to the house, calling out 'Bridget, Bridget, come to my house, come to my house tonight, open the door to Bridget, and let Bridget come in'. When these words had been said the rushes were carefully laid on the floor as a carpet or bed for the saint.[11]

A more elaborate Candlemas Eve ritual took place in the Western Isles of Scotland. A sheaf of oats was dressed up in woman's clothes and put in a large basket called Bride's bed. A wooden club was put beside the basket and when that was done the women of the household called out, 'Briid is come. Briid is welcome.' This was done just before everyone went to bed. When they got up in the morning, the women looked at the ashes of the fire to see whether they had been disturbed by the club. If nothing was found that could indicate that the spirit of Briid had been active in the house during the night, then the auguries for the coming year were bad; but if there was any sign that she had picked up the club, everyone expected that fortune would smile on the coming harvest.

In the next chapter I shall discuss how the religion of the Celts melded with that of the Roman invaders who settled here for three hundred years; but first I should like to leap ahead and take a brief look at what the medieval romancers made of the Celtic winter

Bridestones Long Barrow, Staffordshire

festivals. In Welsh literature we find that the magician, bard and prophet, Taleisin, was born of the witch Ceridwen at mid-winter, and that in later life he boasted that he had witnessed both the fall of Lucifer and the birth of Christ. Irish legend has it that the Druid, Cathbad was careful to arrange that his son Conchobar, who is alleged to have ruled Ulster at the beginning of the Christian era, should be born at the very moment of Christ's nativity.

In England, whatever Druidic rites went on at the solstice seem to have crystallised into the stories about King Arthur and the court he held at this time of year. The most notable of these is the Mercian tale of *Sir Gawain and the Green Knight*. According to the medieval scholar, Jessie Weston (on whose work on the Grail legend T.S. Eliot based *The Waste Land*), Gawain was a solar divinity whose strength waxed and waned as the day advanced. She made her point from Malory's words, which tell how: 'Sir Gawayne/fro it passed nine of the clock waxed ever stronger and stronger for thenne hit came to the hour of noone/ and thryse his myghte was encreased/ And then it was past noone/ and when it drewe toward evensong Syre Gawayne's strength febled and waxst passynge faint that unnethe he might dure any lenger'.

Gawain's opponent in the story was the Green Knight. He drew his strength from the powerful fertilising force of nature, and was even able to lose his head without being killed. He is made up of all the luxuriant green men with foliate heads from Puck to Hob of the wild woods who have ever appeared in English folklore, and he is also connected with the fairies who lived among the long barrows; for it is at such a place, a green chapel, that Gawain is forced to meet him twelve months and a day after their original encounter.

The head of the Green Knight is the central part of this story. For the early Celts were head-hunters, like many other primitive people, and they raised the cult of the severed human head to a pivot of their religion. They believed that it still possessed the power of thought and the vision that it had had in life, and that it could be endowed with speech. So it is quite reasonable that in the medieval story the severed head of the Green Knight should be capable of giving instructions to Gawain, the representative of the Sun God, who is to hold power during the coming year. The fact that the Green Knight's head is cut off at Arthur's Christmas feast is also significant, for Dr Anne Ross records that 'Several heroic or divine characters are referred to as never sitting down at a feast without having a severed head before them on the table'.[13]

Although the story of Gawain relates to Christmas and the solstice, feasts such as the one on which the Green Knight intruded must originally have taken place after the sacrifices of Samhain and Imbolc. It was the Romans, with their Saturnalia, who once again established the solstice as the main feast of winter.

References:
1. ANNE ROSS: *Everyday Life of the Pagan Celts*, Batsford, 1970
2. W.Y. EVANS-WENTZ: *The Fairy Faith in Celtic Countries*, Henry Frowde, 1911
3. ANNE ROSS: *Everyday Life of the Pagan Celts*, Transworld, 1972
4. JAMES MCKAY writing in *The Malvern Advertiser*, 1875
5. VOPISCUS: *Numerians xiv, Aurelianus xliii 4.5*, quoted by Anne Ross
6. For fuller studies of the Celtic religion *see* STUART PIGGOT: *The Druids*, Thames & Hudson, 1968; T.G.E. POWELL: *The Celts*, Thomas & Hudson, 1958
7. ANNE ROSS: *Everyday Life of the Pagan Celts*, Transworld, 1972
8. D.W. HARDING: *The Iron Age in Lowland Britain*, Routledge & Kegan Paul, 1974
9. OWEN'S *Welsh Dictionary*
10. W. CAREW HAZLITT: *Popular Antiquities of Great Britain*, 1870, based on collections recorded by the eighteenth-century antiquarian John Brand
11. A.W. MOORE: *The Folklore of the Isle of Man*, Brown & Son, Douglas, 1891
12. ANNE ROSS: *Everyday Life of the Pagan Celts*

3 ♦ THE ROMANS: FROM SATURNALIA TO CHRISTMAS

> Mithras, God of the Midnight, here where the great bull dies
> Look on thy children in darkness. Oh take our sacrifice!
> Many roads thou has fashioned: all of them lead to the Light,
> Mithras, also a soldier, teach us to die aright!
>
> RUDYARD KIPLING, from *Puck of Pook's Hill*

The Roman occupation of Britain, like the dawn of Christianity which coincided with it, marked a watershed in the religious rites and ceremonies of these islands. During those centuries many disparate threads tangled together and in trying to trace their individual course it is not always possible to keep to a strict chronological order. After the establishment of the early church in the third and fourth centuries there was an open conflict between the pagan rites of the winter solstice and the ceremonies belonging to Christianity.

Before that time, religious ceremonies were dominated by the complex and sophisticated rituals established by the Druids, which gradually mingled with the worship of Roman gods. That was no simple matter, for although the Roman legions eventually adopted one god Mithras, as the focal point of their religion, when they first came to Britian they brought with them a pantheon as numerous and far more orderly than that which ruled the destinies of the Celts. In the early years of the first century AD, the state religion of Rome was based on worship of the Unconquered Sun assisted by a bureaucracy of deities, each one of which presided over a carefully allocated department of life.

'It is expedient that there should be gods,' Ovid wrote, in justification of religious institutions whose sole function was to enable the state to maintain law and order. This arid system worked because it was wisely balanced by the safety valve of the public festivals. Chief among these was the Saturnalia which replaced the earlier winter festival of the Brumalia.

The Saturnalia, which was held at the time of the winter solstice, took the form of a week-long feast in which everything was turned upside down: masters waited on their servants and even the strict laws against gambling were relaxed. The revelry was so noisy and exuberant that Pliny was driven to the expedient of building himself a soundproof room for the duration of the holiday.

Saturn, to whom the festival was dedicated, was an agricultural deity, thought to have got his name from the Latin *satus*, sowing. His feast began on 17 December, and from the time of Augustus it included two days, 19 and 20 December, which were particularly sacred to his wife Ops. The main tradition that we have inherited from it is our custom of exchanging gifts at mid-winter. Like us, the Romans gave presents as tokens of affection to friends and relations, and also as a part of the general expectations of official and business life. In Rome, a client relied on his patron to give him a new toga each December as well as a substantial amount of silver ware.[1] In his turn, the client marked Saturnalia by giving his children little clay dolls called *sigillaria*, which were later replaced by more sophisticated toys.

A purely ritual exchange of gifts was practised by devotees of the woodland goddess, Strenia. They presented each other with twigs cut in her sacred grove in a ceremony that was supposed to bring good fortune to all who took part in it. This became a New Year function in which sacred twigs from the grove of the goddess at Strenia were carried along the Via Sacra. After the procession, the consuls who were embarking on their year of office presented diplomatic gifts known as *strenae*.

The game of hiding coins and small trinkets in the Christmas pudding is another winter custom we have inherited from the Romans, who adopted similar methods of casting lots with food to see who should be king of festival or lord of misrule. Like the charred cake of the Celts, this method of picking out one individual was once the way the sacrificial victim was selected. Like the new sun, the one who drew the lot would rule for a period of twelve months and, like the sun, he had to die the following winter.

By the time the Romans came to Britain any form of human sacrifice was well in the past. The empty and mostly harmless formalities of the state religious rites were sufficient for most people just as a 'C of E' registration is today for the majority of British citizens. Yet some have never been so easily content, and at the height of its imperial power Rome began to experience a religious turmoil comparable to our own new age awakening with its introduction of exotic philosophies from the east.

In Italy that process had started in the third century BC, when an esoteric cult was formed to worship the Phrygian fertility goddess Cybele. In the secret rites of this Great Mother the young god Attis figured as her acolyte and consort. His story runs parallel to those of Adonis and Aphrodite, Isis and Osiris. Each year he was born at the winter solstice, and each year as the days shortened, he died.

Like many secret religions, that cult gradually became more widely practised, and was in turn replaced by a publicly recognised religion that could be put to the social use of maintaining the administrative hierarchy. The new religion which grew out of the rites of Attis was Mithraism. Like his predecessor, Mithras was born at mid-winter, but unlike him he fought against the powers of darkness instead of succumbing to them. For this reason he was adopted by soldiers, and those who followed him vowed to take arms with him against Ahriman, prince of destruction. These vows caused no conflict with the initiate's duty to the state, and so Mithraism had official blessing. This was the religion the Roman army brought to Britain along with the multitudinous deities of the classical pantheon.

It had started as a heresy of the Zoroastrianism which flourished in Iran during the seventh century BC. According to that heretical sect, Mithras was the mediator between Ahriman, who was imagined in human form with the head of a gaping lion and with a serpent entwined round his body, and Horomazes, the god of light. At the winter sunrise, when the birth of Mithras was celebrated, his function as a fertility god was established by the slaying of a white bull. In Britain, the victim was probably one of the great white beasts with pinkish brown ears which were known to be sacred in Roman times and which still exist in carefully recorded herds in Norfolk and Northumberland. The bull was killed because Mithras, unlike Attis, did not have to die in order that the ground should blossom again. That miracle was accomplished through the blood of the slaughtered animal. In some versions of the story the bull was not killed by Mithras but by Ahriman, in an attempt to bring all life on earth to an end. His plan was frustrated, for the creature's brain and inner organs fertilised the ground they fell on; while his seed, which was carried to the moon for purification, engendered all the animals on earth. Only the wolves and the cat tribe remained in Ahriman's power.

Whether the bull was killed by Mithras or by Ahriman, its death took place in a cave, which resembled the birthplace of the god. For Mithras sprang fully grown from the rocks of his mother earth, accompanied by twin torch bearers, Cautes who represented the spring and the rising sun and who held his torch aloft, and Cautopates whose torch was held downwards to represent sunset and autumn. Only a group of shepherds witnessed this miraculous event; but the cave, like the cave/stable of Bethlehem where shepherds also witnessed a miraculous birth, became part of the mid-winter ritual. The remains of the Mithraic temple at Housesteads on Hadrian's wall indicate a cave sanctuary; and it has been argued that the oddly named hamlet of Cave Gate to the east of Buntigford in Hertfordshire was once associated with the bull sacrifice of Mithras.

Early in the first century AD Pliny claimed that the cult of Mithras was enthusiastically adopted by many of the Celts, after their Druids had been massacred by Caesar's invading forces. 'Britain is still fascinated by magic,' he wrote, 'and performs its rites with so much ceremony that it almost seems as though it was she who imported the cult to the Persians.' Nor was it only the cult of Mithras that the Celts adopted; for the Romans brought with them other and more powerful secret mysteries relating to Apollo and Dionysius, two gods who were both supposed to have been born at mid-winter. Apollo was often equated with Maponus or Mabon, whom the northern Celts honoured as a patron of youth and music and one of whose temples the Romans preserved at Ribchester in the south Pennines. The classical Apollo, god of harmony, music and health, was never native to Rome. He was adopted originally from Greece, and then sometimes ascribed to Britain, which was equated with the legendary country of the Hyperboreans, the worshippers of Apollo who dwelt beyond the north wind.

Dionysius also came to Rome from the Greek pantheon, although his worship originated in Asia. His rituals, which included orgiastic

The Romans: from Saturnalia to Christmas ♦ 35

celebrations by drunken women, were never encouraged by the authorities; but official condemnation only strengthened their powerful attraction for those who saw these rites as part of the worship of the Great Mother; for the Celts, as Dr Anne Ross[2] points out, were much given to cults of powerful female deities.

The rituals of all these gods contributed to the celebration of the winter solstice in Roman Britain. But if the Roman authorities hoped that by arranging for the festival of Saturnalia to come to an end before the first day of January, the month dedicated to the god of doorways and fresh starts, they would get the people in sober mood to start the next year's work, they were badly frustrated. For just as our legislators recently had to submit to the facts of public behaviour and declare 1 January a holiday, so did the Romans come to accept that the start of another year would be greeted with public merrymakings on a scale that rivalled the orgies of mid-winter.

Before Mithras was adopted by the army a white bull had been sacrificed by the Romans at the start of the year. That offering was made to Jupiter, great father of the gods, both as a thanks offering for the preceding year and as a pledge for the coming twelve months, each one of which had its special altar in the temple of Janus, the two-headed leader of the gods. Naturally this was an occasion for divination, largely undertaken by scrutinising the entrails of the sacrificed beast. The Romans made up for their lack of real instinct for religion by the zeal with which they invented methods of forecasting the future and the trust they put in the omens. It is a trait we share, for although we may have become too squeamish to prod around in the liver and lights of slaughtered animals in order to discover our fortunes, we have readily adopted the cleaner, if more mathematically demanding, method of astrology as an indication of future events.

That is no new thing. The history of astrology is as old as religion itself. When men first devised ways to worship and placate the gods they thought to be in charge of men's destinies, they had their eyes on the heavens and related the patterns of the stars to events on earth. We know from the alignments of their stone circles that Bronze Age men were astute astronomers, and although we have no record of them as astrologers, it seems reasonable to suppose that they too recognised constellations that in some way corresponded to the zodiacal effigies with which we are familiar. Certainly as trade with the Mediterranean was so well established throughout the Iron Age, the Celts of Britain must have had some notion of the twelve classical signs of the zodiac before the Romans brought them here. There are three winter creatures: Scorpio, who 'fights against the sun' as T.S. Eliot wrote in *East Coker*; Sagittarius, centaur and archer; and Capricorn, the fish-tailed god with his horn of plenty for the coming year. Of these, the solstice figure of Sagittarius has always been the most important. The centaur can be seen as the man horse who pulled the chariot of the sun; for the Celts the figure could well have had a resemblance to Epona; and even in Christian times it was such a vital symbol that we find a Sagittarius carved in the church of Hook Norton in the Cotswolds.

Sagittarius

Folklore is full of devices for telling the future at the start of the new year. Some of these, like the tradition of St Agnes Eve, may be a domestic inheritance of the public casting of the omens practised by the Roman administrators during the first month of the year. St Agnes was martyred under Diocletian at the age of thirteen; her day falls on 21 January, and the night before was a popular time for looking into the future. In the seventeenth century, John Aubrey wrote of St Agnes Eve, 'you take a row of pins and pull everyone, one after another saying a Pater Noster, sticking a pin in your sleeve, and you will dream of him or her you shall marry.'

That minor example is part of a more vital thread of continuity. For just as the Roman rituals carried many Celtic traditions forward, they also coloured future Christian practices. This happened

The Romans: from Saturnalia to Christmas ♦ 37

even though Caesar's legions waged a bitter and desperate war against the Druids while later Roman administrators persecuted the Christians because their religious loyalties, unlike those of the followers of Mithras, were felt to run counter to their duties to the state.

When Christianity eventually replaced Mithraism as the acceptable religion of Rome, the persecution was switched to those who would not give up their pagan beliefs. So after 306 AD, when the Emperor Constantine made Christianity the official religion of the Empire, it was said that all pagan rites were so fiercely attacked that people were scared to so much as look at the sunset. Yet even while the missionaries spread the new religion throughout Britain, we can be sure that many of the old seasonal festivals remained. Successive popes and bishops encouraged the building of Christian churches on pagan sites so that people could continue to worship in places they were accustomed to hold sacred and attempted to Christianise the pagan festivals by fitting them into the Church calendar.

Yet there is no doubt that the pagan rites continued, for even as the first churches were being set up in England at Glastonbury and Canterbury, the temples which served both Celtic and Roman gods were being widely extended. This came about through the revival of pagan cults instigated by Julian the Apostate's declaration of religious freedom. This must have done much to keep the old Celtic festivals alive, for it is an interesting coincidence that it was during the season of Samhain (6 November of the year 355 AD) that the augurs deemed the time auspicious for Julian to be created Caesar; and it was around Imbolc (4 February 362 AD) that he made his famous declaration. It was after that that the Celtic temple of Nodens at Lydney in Gloucestershire was splendidly rebuilt with guest house, baths, dormitories and meditation rooms, all designed for visiting pilgrims, who may well have come to the temple for the major seasonal festivals.

This was not the only Celtic temple to be adopted by the Romans or used for the worship of their own gods. They built a temple at Frilford, where, as we have already seen, the Celts worshipped on the site of a Neolithic shrine and another was incorporated with the Celtic temple among the ramparts of Maiden Castle. In many other places a Christian church eventually came to stand on sites which had been sacred to both Romans and Celts. We can be sure that the rites that took place in and around these Romano-British temples before the arrival of the Christian missionaries, were based on the worship of the sun and rituals designed to increase the fertility of man, beast and corn. Some form of Samhain festival may have formed part of the ceremonies connected with these temples. They would have combined well with the feast of Jupiter, which was celebrated in mid-November. At that season sacrificial animals were eaten and two weeks of Plebian games were held from 4 to 17 November. Later the Romans gave 11 November, the date of their ancient vintage feast, to their most cherished Christian, St Martin, a fourth-century Bishop of Tours.

In some ways Martin was a very British saint. He was particularly beloved by that Maximus who was proclaimed emperor by the legions in Britain and who was both romanticised and canonised by Welsh and Cornish writers of the early middle ages as Saint Mascen. It is likely that some of the rites of Samhain, and many of the festivals associated with the Roman November games, which were still being held in the fourth century AD, were made respectable as part of the celebration of Martinmas.

I have found that it is worthwhile looking at the site of any church which has been dedicated to that saint. Very often it stands on ground that has been sacred for millennia. The best known and the oldest of all the St Martin's churches stands just outside the east walls of Canterbury. It was there when St Augustine came to Kent and at the end of the seventh century Bede described it as 'a church built of ancient time in honour of St Martin, made while the Romans were yet dwelling in Britain'.[3] The west wall of the present building is claimed to be one of the most ancient in Britain, and is certainly one of the most beautiful, being made of Roman bricks infilled with rubble that was probably part of the Celtic temple that stood here before the Romans came.

It was not only in the temples that the Romans worshipped. Like the Celts who practised the old rites of their seasonal festivals in their farms and homesteads right up to the nineteenth century, the Romans observed religious ceremonies in their villas. The deities portrayed on some of the floor mosaics (I think particularly of the panels relating to Orpheus at Littlecote Park near Hungerford) indicate that it was the sun to which these family prayers were indirectly addressed.

The Romans: from Saturnalia to Christmas ♦ 39

St Martin's Church, Canterbury

At the great feasts, the religious ceremonies burst the bounds of both villa and temple. It happened in the November games at the time of the sacrifice to Jupiter, again throughout the Saturnalia and in early February, when torch and candlelight processions heralded the feast of Februa, mother of Mars, and the fertility rites of the Lupercalia. At such a time the Celts could well have celebrated Imbolc unremarked. In any case, Bride, the goddess who presided over it, was adopted by the Romans in her northern guise of Brigantia and given Minerva's spear and shield. Later, as we have seen, the Church took her over as St Bridget.

Some Roman villas yield evidence in the form of mosaics and artefacts marked with the Chi-ro symbol, that the inhabitants were in fact Christians; and there are references to Christians in Rome celebrating the birth of Christ at the time of the winter solstice from the second century; but it was not until the end of the ninth century, when the Saturnalia must have been well forgotten, that King Alfred declared that Christmas should be kept as a twelve-day feast.

From that time the annual winter holiday ended in a festival reminiscent of the Roman Compitalia, which was held early in January to mark the end of the farming year. For Christians it was Plough Monday, kept on the first Monday after Twelfth Night. (There is more about this in Chapter 6 and 8.) The Roman Compitalia was held at a place where four estates or small holdings met. A little shrine was erected in such a manner that it was open in all four directions. This meant that the presiding god of each estate could enter it. A plough was set up on one of the four altars in this shrine, and with it a wooden doll for every free person in each

Sul-Minerva figurine, Bath

household and a wooden ball for each slave. Clearly the custom was partly borrowed from the solstice gifts of *sigillaria*. But before the Church had a chance to take over this ritual in Britain, together with all the others I have described in this chapter, it was to suffer a sea change at the hands of the Saxon pirates.

References:
1. JEROME CARCOPINO: *Daily Life in Ancient Rome*, Routledge & Kegan Paul, 1941, quoting Martial, Books V and VII
2. ANNE ROSS: *Everyday Life of the Pagan Celts*, Batsford, 1970
3. VENERABLE BEDE: *Ecclesiastical History of the English Nation*, Book I, Chapter xxvi, 113

Other general sources for this chapter are:
PETER D. ARNOTT: *An Introduction to the Roman World*, Macmillan, 1970
R.M. OGILVIE: *The Romans and their Gods*, Chatto & Windus, 1969
R.C. ZAEHNER: *The Dawn and Twilight of Zoroastrianism*, Weidenfeld & Nicolson, 1975

4 ♦ YULETIDE: THE GODS OF THE NORTH

> I know I hung
> on the windswept Tree,
> through nine days and nights.
> I was stuck with a spear
> and given to Odin
> myself given to myself.

Havamal, a poem in *The Edda* translated by D.E. MARTIN CLARKE, Cambridge University Press, 1923

Right through the Dark Ages in Britain, the worship of Odin in one form or another contended with that of Christ. Even though Christianity overcame Mithraism as the state religion during the Roman occupation; and even though the Celtic saints built churches on

Reconstruction of Saxon huts, West Stow, Bury St. Edmunds

many of the old sacred sites, a new form of paganism came into the country with the Anglo-Saxon settlers, who finally turned a large part of Britain into England by their decisive victories over the Celts at the end of the sixth century. During the next three hundred years, many of these Saxons officially became Christian, but their new and uncertain faith was rapidly shaken by fresh hordes of Viking invaders. Then their old Teutonic god Woden, with his mid-winter festival of Yule, was reinstated in the terrible form of the Norse Odin. It was his worshippers that the Christian Alfred struggled against in the ninth century; and when the Danelaw was established, it was to Odin that the people made their sacrifices at the time of the winter solstice.

We know a little of how the festival of Yule was celebrated in northern Scandinavia from a Roman writer, Procopius,[1] who described how those people divided the long dark winters. He tells us that when the Scandinavians in the far north had been thirty-five days without sunlight, they sent scouts to the mountaintops to look for the return of the sun. When the first glimmer of returning light was seen, the scouts took the good news into the valleys, and immediately the great festival of the year began. Farther south the period of darkness was shorter so that the solstice feast varied in its timing and duration according to the latitude. In England, where we never lose the sun completely, there must have been some more subtle way of knowing exactly when the year had turned and the great rejoicing could begin.

Scholars generally agree that Yuletide, like the Roman Saturnalia, lasted about two weeks, but that the actual season of Yule went on far longer, running from mid-November to the end of January. In that way it was similar to the Celtic period from Samhain to Imbolc. The derivation of the name of the feast is still elusive. The best explanation I have come across claims that the word 'Yule' stems from the same root as 'wheel'; and that this disc refers both to the sun and to the chariot of the great god, Woden or Odin. The word can also mean a loud shout, and in that sense it was at some time Christianised by the custom of crying 'Yole' in church at the end of the Christmas Day service. In Yorkshire that tradition was kept up into the seventeenth century.

We have to turn to the Norse sagas of the eleventh century for accounts of the traditional celebration of Yule. Their descriptions of the lavish feasting that took place in mid-winter in Iceland and Norway probably bear a fair resemblance to the 'Yule biddings and drink bouts'[2] that went on in the mead halls of the Saxon lords in England. The folklorist and Scandinavian scholar Hilda Davidson describes such a boat-shaped hall, which was excavated in northern Iceland in 1908.[3] Like the hall which forms part of the setting for the seventh-century Anglo-Saxon epic poem of *Beowulf*, this one had a long fire pit down the centre, with additional hearths at either end. There were raised sections for seats facing the fire and other places for the lesser warriors, who had to put up with the cold and face the side walls. Only men took part in the great banquets in the mead halls, although noble ladies might sometimes briefly attend them. Dr Davidson estimates that the Icelandic hall could have accommodated 150 warriors. She also thinks that the building served as a temple as well as a hall, in which case it would be used for both the Yuletide feasts and the autumn sacrifices.

By the time the sagas were written down many of the Yuletide revellers were superficially Christians, although they still surreptitiously practised the old rites. In one saga a messenger is compelled to tell Olaf the Holy,[4] 'This is the truth to tell, King, if I am to tell things as they are, throughout Upper Thrandheim, well nigh all the folk are all-heathen in their faith, though some men be there who are christened. Now it is their wont to have a blood offering in autumn to welcome the winter, and another at mid-winter.'

Up to the beginning of the ninth century, the sagas of the Kings of Norway are full of descriptions of these late autumn festivals and sacrifices, although they make little mention of Yule, and what went on in a modified form throughout tenth-century Iceland, certainly took place openly in the pagan parts of England, where the Norse rites of winter were practised. The Venerable Bede (*c*.673–735) wrote of November as *Blotmonath* or Blood-month, so called because of the great slaughter of cattle that took place at this time. Blood offerings were also made in February, when the days begin to lengthen noticeably, at a time that corresponds to the Celtic Imbolc and the Christian Candlemas. Bede knew that season as Solmonath, when the pagan Saxons offered sol (little cakes) to the gods.

But although the early Anglo-Saxon settlers in England held these late autumn and early spring ceremonies, it is the mid-winter sacrifice to Woden, or Odin, and the feasting that accompanied it, which have left the greatest marks on our traditions. Odin, who was born of a union between the god Bor and the giantess Bestla, descended to earth on a white horse at the sacred season of Yule. In all his rites he is associated with horses, both as the driver of a chariot drawn by the mighty eight-footed Sleipnir, whose teeth were engraved with letters of the runic script that the god created, and as the recipient of horse sacrifices. Nor was Odin content with animal offerings. The bloody ravens that surmounted the standards the Danes carried into battle have been taken as an indication of human sacrifice to Odin.

When the Christian church set out to defeat the old gods by turning them into devils, Odin, as leader of the Wild Hunt or Asgards Reid was the most fearful of all. All over England, from Peterborough to Dartmoor, folk tales persist of his dreaded, demonic horsemen pursuing human souls to their doom. In the Middle Ages, when people heard the baying of dogs in the frosty nights of mid-winter they crossed themselves in dread, for they took it as a sign that Odin, with his disembodied spirits, was out hunting to kill. Even those who put their trust in the cross regularly took the precaution of leaving one last sheaf of corn rotting in the field after harvest to placate the god and his ravenous steed.

The eight-legged Sleipnir is taken to represent four men carrying a bier, which is why the association with death is so strong. Dr Davidson makes this point by quoting Verrier Elwin's translation of a funeral dirge used among the Gonds in India and referring to the eight-legged horse Bagri Maro:

> What horse is this?
> It is the horse Bagri Maro.
> What should we say of its legs?
> The horse has eight legs.
> What should we say of its heads?
> The horse has four heads . . .
> Catch the bridle and mount the horse.[5]

Those words could well fit Sleipnir. The last line takes the concept farther: the eight-legged horse was not only a token of death, it was also the steed on which a shaman could ride between the worlds of the living and the dead. Dr Davidson makes a strong case for considering that many of Odin's attributes are those associated with the practice of shamanism in Asia and north-east Europe. Like those priestly magicians he was supposed to be able to change his shape and take the form of a bird of prey, or fly through the air mounted on horseback. His travels took him to other worlds; but he was also represented as constantly travelling in this one. For that reason Odin, like his Roman counterpart Mercury, was associated with trade. Like Mercury too, the Norse god is sometimes pictured with a winged hat, although in his case it was more of a hood. The old Norse word grim means simply a hooded man, and in this sense it became synonymous with Odin. Its present meaning arose out of the dread that god inspired, and all the grims-dykes and -ditches of England, as well as Grimes Graves, are named for the devil in Odin's guise.

Out of this grim god we have made Father Christmas. Rogan Taylor[6] has shown how that benevolent old gentleman in his cheery red dressing gown was derived from the Siberian shamans who intoxicated themselves into illusions of flying by eating the red spotted fungus, fly agaric, an addiction shared by the reindeer. The practice extended to Lapland and was no doubt familiar to the Norse Vikings who brought Odin to England. They would also have the idea of the shaman descending into a house by a hole in the roof, for the winter dwellings in Siberia are underground like the North Americans' kivas referred to in Chapter 1. Like the kivas, these underground dwellings were entered by a hole in the roof above the fireplace. Our modern Santa Claus has Sleipnir multiplied into a team of reindeer, while the god's prerogative of judging the deeds of men has been humanised into the benevolent practice of rewarding good children.

Odin was undoubtedly the greatest of the Norse gods, and the one who has left the heaviest imprint on our traditions, folklore and place names; but other Scandinavian deities are still with us in various forms. There is Odin's son Thunor or Thor, worshipped up to the eleventh century by the Vikings in Dublin. His mother was the primeval earth goddess Nerthus, and from her he gained his power over the weather, which made him the patron of agriculture.

Thor is usually depicted as a red-bearded young man of enormous strength and appetites. He is shown either brandishing his axe or travelling in a chariot pulled by goats. Like the Roman Mithras, he was doomed to fight annually with the powers of evil and destruction. In his case the dark forces were symbolised by the serpent Ragnorak, or Nidhogg, who threatened one of the three roots of Yggdrasil, the tree of life. The other two were constantly under attack from the frost giants and from the freezing northern fogs of Niffheim. Thor's fight with the serpent is a typical solar myth, though it belongs to the beginning of winter rather than to the solstice. The god, who takes nine paces in his march towards the foe, is temporarily killed and lies dead for the winter months. We can take each of his advancing paces to represent the months of spring, summer and autumn. By the time the Danes came to settle in England, Thor had superseded his father as the most popular of the gods, and so became the chief opponent of Christ. Yet the two eventually came together. The Gosfirth Cross in Cumbria, which was carved at the beginning of the tenth century, shows Thor fishing for the great serpent using a bull's head as bait.

Far more cheerful than either Odin or Thor were the twin deities Freyr and Freyja. Freyr was the god of the golden sunshine, whose image was taken to the winter feasts; and Freyja, the goddess of fertility, was like Odin in that she could travel in the form of a bird. Both these two were associated with the cult of the boar, and it is to them we owe the now almost completely vanished tradition of eating a boar's head as a part of the Christmas feast. The Vikings sacrificed a boar to Freyr at Yule, and according to the seventeenth-century writer, John Aubrey 'a boar's head with a lemon in its mouth' was the first dish of Christmas up to the time of the Civil War.

Freyr and Freyja represented love, peace and goodwill as well as fertility. Freyr's sword was made out of the flashing rays of the sun, and he used it to fight against the frost giants. Wherever he went he was accompanied by Schrimir, the sacred, golden-bristled boar, who could run more swiftly than the sun of which he was an emblem. As such, and as a sign of regeneration and protection, the boar was carried by the standard bearers into war and used as an adornment for the helmets of the warriors. Descriptions of such boar emblems are to be found in *Beowulf*; and the actual object has been discovered in archaeological excavations such as the Sutton Hoo ship burial in East Anglia, where a boar adorns the cheek guard of the helmet; and the barrow at Benty Grange near Monyash in

Sutton Hoo helmet

Derbyshire, where a helmet, now displayed in the Sheffield City Museum, is protected both by Freyr's boar and Christ's cross.

The most delightful of the Norse deities was Odin's wife Frigg. She appears to have been his consort although his son Thor was begotten on Nerthus. We remember Frigg in the name of the sixth day of the week, which in other countries is called for her counterpart, Venus. She, rather than Nerthus, was thought of as being the mother of the gods, but the genealogies of these northern deities are as confused as those of the Celts, and sometimes we find Frigg described as the daughter of the earth goddess Fiorgynn, an earlier form of Nerthus.

Her appearance at the winter solstice connects her with Balder the Beautiful, who was compelled like Adonis to die in the autumn in order that spring could return. It was Frigg who commanded all nature to weep at Balder's death. The story goes that Balder (who was also a son of Odin) had a prophetic dream which informed him that he should be killed. When he told her of it Frigg made every animal, plant and stone swear to do him no harm. Only the mistletoe did not comply. So it was with that plant that Loki (the evil giant who is said to have fathered Odin's horse Sleipnir) was able to kill the young hero.

This was the pantheon that the Danes brought to Britain, and which lived for some time alongside the Christian hierarchies of the Saxons and Celts. Even when the Danes were converted to Christ in the tenth century, Canute had to issue an edict proclaiming, 'It is heathen for a man to worship idols, that is to worship heathen gods, and the sun or moon, fire or flood, wells or stones, or any kind of trees, or to practise witchcraft or contrive murder by sorcery.'[7] The last clause suggests that the newly converted Christian king felt that pagan magic could be effective.

Canute was by no means the first Christian in England to complain about the heathen practices of his supposedly converted countrymen. The British monk Gildas, writing in the sixth century, deplored 'the diabolical idols of my country, which almost surpassed in number those of Egypt'. A century later, Bede proudly proclaimed of the year 640 that King Earconbert was 'the first King of England, who of his princely authority commanded that the idols in all his whole realm should be forsaken and destroyed,' and he 'appointed meet and convenient punishments for the transgressors thereof.'[8] Despite these measures his edict does not seem to have been wholly successful.

Forty years previously, Pope Gregory had made a more subtle move against the refusal of the old gods to disappear decently. He declared that pagan temples and customs should remain where they were, but be dedicated to Christ. And as we have seen the rites of the solstice were Christianised when it was decreed, in the middle of the fourth century, that Christ's birth should be officially celebrated in mid-December. But it was not until the ninth century that any definite move was made to Christianise the pagan November rituals. In 830 the feast of All Saints was established on 1 November and in 993, 2 November was consecrated as All Souls' Day. Presumably one hundred and sixty years had not proved long enough to wipe out the observances of the pagan ceremonies of the dead that took place at Samhain and at the time of the late autumn sacrifices to Odin, so that the Church had to try again.

It can never have been an easy matter to bring all the heathen winter festivals within the fold of the Church, and it is a task that has never been fully concluded. The early Church was not much interested in Christmas; Bede hardly mentions it. It is Easter that is at the heart of the Christian religion, and it was the date of the observance of that festival that mattered to the Church fathers. When Bede wrote about the pagan festival of the solstice, he ignored Odin and went back to the winter festival of the earth goddess, which he referred to as Mother's Night. The term remained, for a contributor to *The Gentleman's Magazine* for 1748 reminded his readers that 'the night of the winter solstice was called by our ancestors, Mother Night, as they reckoned the beginning of their years from then'.

Mother Night was also usually taken as the beginning of each year by the monks who compiled the *Anglo-Saxon Chronicle*, although they naturally referred to it as Christmas. These holy scribes were quite ready to admit the existence of Odin/Woden, as, for example in their description of the Saxon Cerdic, who invaded Britain in 494; he was the 'the son of Gewis, the son of Wig, the son of Freawine, the son of Frithugar, the son of Brand, the son of Bældæg, the son of Woden.'[9]

As for the actual Christmas entries, the Parker manuscript chronicles an eclipse of the moon on Christmas morning of the year 827. That is a little confusing, as by our reckoning that eclipse happened at 2 am on 25 December 828, which the chroniclers would probably have entered as 829.

It is the entry for 1131, however, which takes the natural events of winter into the realms of magic and folklore. In that year the omens were dreadful, for 'after Christmas, on a Sunday night at first sleep, the sky in the north was all as if it was a burning fire, so that all who saw it were afraid as they had never been before – that was 11 January. In the course of the same year, there was such a great cattle plague all over England as had never been before in the memory of man – that was among cattle and pigs, so that in a village that had 10 or 12 ploughs in action, there was not one left, and the man who had two hundred or three hundred pigs had not one left. After that, the hens died, then the meat and cheese and butter ran short. May God amend it when it is his will!'[10]

If established Christians could hint that such disasters were connected with strange phenomena in the sky, it is not surprising that the traditions of Yule should have left their mark so strongly on semi-pagan people in fairly remote places. These traditions went into folk tales as well as into the customs of the season. One of the Yuletide stories collected by the brothers Grimm concerns the tradition that, on the eve of Yule, the long-lived giants who had been turned to stone could be brought back to life for the space of seven hours if one of their own race embraced them. That kiss cost the living giant one hundred years of his or her lifespan.

In the Shetland Isles, which, like Orkney, bear many traces of their long Norse occupation, the complicated Yule festivities were haunted by the presence of giants and of the trows (or trolls), the little people who live in underground caves. Tul'ya's E'en, which was celebrated seven days before the solstice, was a particularly vulnerable time for ordinary people. So a special 'Saining' had to be held to protect men and women from the bewitching powers of the fairy world, and to save the children from being taken as changelings. As a thank offering for having got their children safely through that perilous time, their grateful parents rededicated them to the Virgin Mary on the following night, Helya's Night.

In Orkney the trows were thought to be particularly dangerous on the night of 24 December, when they surrounded the crofts waiting to turn the quern stones, moving them widdershins against the sun. According to the Orkney poet George Mackay Brown,[11] that would render the stones barren and prevent the flour giving any nourishment to the family. To frustrate this trick the crofters' wives moved the upper quern stones from the lower for this one night of the year.

Because of its latitude, and because of the old Norse custom of allowing a long stretch of time either side of the solstice for the Yule festival, Yuletide in Shetland lasted for twenty-four days rather than for our more familiar twelve. Until the eighteenth century each Sunday of that period was devoted to merrymaking held in a different house each week. While the eve of St Thomas's Day (20

Up Helly Aa, the burning of the Viking ship, Shetland

December) was considered too holy for work of any kind.

The Sunday before Christmas was called Byana's Sunday, the day on which half a cow's head was boiled and eaten for supper. Afterwards the skull was carefully cleaned and a candle stuck in the eye socket. On Christmas morning the head of the household lit this candle before giving his animals a special feed.

As Shetland did not adopt the new style calendar until 1879, the last night of the old year was celebrated on 10 January (our dating) and the holiday ended on 29 January, known as Up Helly Aa (the end of the holiday), the twenty-fourth day of Yule. In 1889, the practice of marking this time by a great carnival culminating in the burning of a Viking ship was introduced.

References:
1. PROCOPIUS: *Bellum Gothicum*, Book II, Chapter 15
2. SNORRI STURLUSON: *Heimskringla*, translated by E. Monsen and A.H. Smith, Heffer, 1931
3. H.R. ELLIS DAVIDSON: *Pagan Scandinavia*, Thames & Hudson, 1967

4. *The Story of Olaf the Holy*, Chapter cxv
5. VERRIER ELWIN: *The Muria and their Ghotul*, Oxford, 1947; quoted by H.R. Ellis Davidson: *Gods and Myths of Northern Europe*, Penguin 1964
6. ROGAN TAYLOR, *Sunday Times* feature, 21 December 1980
7. The fifth law of Canute, quoted by BRIAN BRANSTON: *Lost Gods of England*, Thames & Hudson, 1957
8. VENERABLE BEDE, *Ecclesiastical History of the English Nation*, Book III, Chapter viii
9. *Anglo-Saxon Chronicle*, translated by G.N. Garmonsway, Everyman, Dent, 1953
10. *Anglo-Saxon Chronicle*, translated by Dorothy Whitlock, Eyre & Spottiswoode, 1962
11. GEORGE MACKAY BROWN: *An Orkney Tapestry*, Quartet, 1973

5 ♦ FIRE AND LIGHT

Bryng in fyre on alhalawgh day,
To condulmas even, I dare welle say
Of grome of halle, or ellis his knafe

The Boke of Curtasye 1430–1440, Early English Text Society, 1868

Up Helly Aa is performed by competing teams of young men who have worked on their various theatrical effects all year and culminates in the burning of a Viking boat. Although that custom was not introduced until the late nineteenth century, it is fitting that a fire festival should mark the end of the Christmas holiday. For obvious practical reasons, rituals of fire and light have always been an essential part of winter ceremonies.

Even as our large offices and institutional buildings reckon to run their central heating systems from November to May, whatever the weather; so the medieval lords organised the winter comfort of their squires and retainers according to defined dates. There were many variations and refinements on the timing given in *The Boke of Curtasye*. In one case, squires were allowed to have fires during dinner from 1 November to Maundy Thursday, and to receive a daily candle from 1 November to 2 February. By the fifteenth century, and probably much earlier, city lighting was also a matter of concern. In 1416, the Lord Mayor of London decreed that every householder should hang out a lantern with a fresh candle provided nightly from All Hallows to Christmas.

A couple of centuries later, in 1656, a certain John Wardell, realising how inadequate this provision was for the second half of winter, left money in his will for the church wardens of St Botolph, Bishopsgate to arrange for an iron and glass lantern with fresh candles in it to be fixed at the north-east corner of the church from the feast of St Bartholomew (31 October) to Lady Day (2 February) – although to be precise 31 October was the date of St Bartholomew's Fair, his actual feast day was 24 August.

During the winter months, when fire provides the light and heat that are necessary to preserve life, it becomes a substitute for the sun. So in ritual as well as practical ways its use had to be carefully ordered. In analysing fire ceremonies throughout the world, J.G. Frazer in *The Golden Bough* concluded that they had two main purposes. In some instances the fire rituals were performed as sympathetic magic, intended to ensure the return of the sun after the winter solstice; in others the cauterising and purifying aspect of fire was uppermost and the sacred flame was regarded as a means of burning up evil and protecting the good from the supernatural powers of the wicked.[1]

Each of the four winter months has its fire ritual or feast of light. November has the fires of All Hallows and Martinmas, which are in direct descent from the Samhain fires of the Celts; December, those of the solstice rituals; in January we find equal importance given to the fires of the New Year and those of Twelfth Night; and February starts off with Candlemas. Many of the fires kindled at these times have a special significance for the coming year. The Hopi Indians of North America can choose either November or February as the month in which to light their New Fire, which is to burn on the central hearth of the tribe throughout the year. Whichever month is chosen, the fire must be lit from the embers of the old one, and the lighting has to be accompanied by a solemn and protracted ceremony enacted only by fully initiated men, who stay in their circular underground kivas for eight days before emerging on the ninth for a public festival.

That Indian ritual corresponds closely to what we know of the Samhain fire festivals of the Iron Age Celts. The chief Druids of Ireland used to meet at Tlachtga, twelve miles from the holy hill of Tara, to kindle the fire on which the sacrifices of Samhain were burnt. On that night, November Eve, all the fires in Ireland had to be put out and then relit from the central fire. For the Celts the tradition of the November fires was so important to the life of the community that it continued right through the Christian era. In the eighth century the Church authorities on the Isle of Man (where 1 November was reckoned as New Year's Day until the eighteenth century) were so concerned at the pagan practice of lighting beacon fires on hilltops at this season that they made serious but unsuccessful attempts to stop the custom. The importance that the people gave to these fires grew out of the belief that their flames had a special vitality which would increase the fertility of cattle who were driven through them, and the strength of young men who leaped over them.

The gift of fertility that came from the November fires was also extended to plants. Well into the nineteenth century, it was quite usual in all parts of Britain for farmers and their families to parade around their fields with torches lit from the Hallowe'en bonfire. They did this in the belief that the flames they carried would increase the fertility of both crops and cattle in the same way as the sun does.

Sympathetic magic apart, the ash that fell from the brands was a token of the systematic fertilising with potash that is scientifically agreed to be beneficial to the soil. Our ancestors were as aware of its properties as are our modern farmers when they set light to the stubble after harvest and as were the pioneer Iron Age cultivators, who prepared new ground for planting by slashing down virgin woodlands and burning the trees and scrub where they fell. Yet practical expediency is only part of the story. In the early years of this century *The Tablet* told its readers of an All Hallows' practice in Lancashire, where 31 October was known as Teanday, a corruption of the Celtic word 'tan' or 'teindh' meaning fire or light. On that day families gathered together and, as a bundle of straw blazed on the prongs of a pitchfork, prayed for the souls of their departed friends. The same tradition inspired the 'Tindles', described in *The Gentleman's Magazine* of 1784 as fires lit on Findern Common in Derbyshire on All Souls' Day for the purpose of lighting souls out of Purgatory.

In Scotland, Samhain fires were lit until the end of the eighteenth century, and there it was the custom for the children to go round begging 'Ge's a peat t'burn the witches',[1] a plea that resembles our 'penny for the guy' and which shares with our own Guy Fawkes tradition the belief that fire at this time has special power to purge evil. The old belief in the potency of the fires also lingered on, for in the parish of Callander, where All Hallow E'en bonfires were set up in every village, it was the custom for each of the boys in turn to lie as near to the fire as he possibly could, allowing the smoke to roll over him while his companions jumped over his prostrate body. Those were not the only uses of the Samhain fires, for they were also used as means of divination, as I have described in Chapter 2.

It is because of the powerful tradition of the Samhain fires, not because we are eager to maintain the authority of Parliament, that it is impossible that the fifth of November 'should ever be forgot'. The question remains as to why one actual, historical figure should be particularly singled out. It has been suggested that Guy Fawkes and his fellow conspirators actually formed a witch coven; and whether that is so or not, it is certain that the seventeenth-century witch-hunting Protestants, who found it convenient to link the land-owning Catholics with Satanic practices, would have given their assent to such a notion. Whatever the historic truth, we can be quite certain that the Guy Fawkes bonfires invoke an ancient custom. The very word 'bonfire' actually derives from bone fire, and is not some Norman French corruption of a 'good fire'. The bones that were burnt were those of the cattle slaughtered at the beginning

Lewes bonfire celebrations, Sussex 1979

Hatherleigh Fire Festival, Devon 1980

of winter, and it was on 'bonfires' that sacrifices to the gods were made.

We still have other local fire ceremonies in early November that are linked in no direct way to the tradition of Guy Fawkes. At Hatherleigh in North Devon, on the evening of the Tuesday nearest to 5 November, tarred barrels are taken into the old market square in the middle of the town, which stands on the slopes of a steep hill. From the moment the festivities begin, men in drag play jazz to the milling crowds, and the local boast is that no-one goes to bed that night. At dusk on the following evening the barrels are put on sledges, set alight and pulled down the main street by the local youths until the new market square at the bottom of the town is reached. Then the carnival gets under way again. A great bonfire is lit and a procession starts led by people carrying flaming torches, who weave their way around an intricate geometric criss-cross pattern. The ceremony ends with the burning of three more tar barrels.

The ancient fires of Samhain which are celebrated at Hatherleigh

Fire and Light ♦ 59

North Somerset pageant

take on a different form in the November festivals of north Somerset. These were instigated at the beginning of this century, and they take place on successive nights in the week following 5 November, the cavalcade moving from town to town from Bridgewater in the west to Shepton Mallet in the east. Each year these carnival processions, made up of a parade of floats illustrating a variety of themes in mime and tableaux, becomes more and more elaborate. This is now more a feast of light than of fire, for each float trails a generator which supplies electricity for massive lighting; but before the First World War, when the floats were farm waggons pulled by horses and torch flares lit the shows, the procession was linked more closely to the rituals of fire.

There is another November feast of the dead which we recall without festival, that is Armistice Day, once strictly observed on 11 November and kept on the nearest Sunday to that date. It is as though the great slaughter of the 1914–18 war had put out the fires of St Martin, whose day this is, and those of the great Teutonic festival of New Year which the Church tried to tame by making the season into Martinmas. That attempt was not completely successful, or perhaps the people's enthusiasm for this saint was too great (*see* Chapter 3 for an account of the way he was venerated by the Romans); for the celebrations of Martinmas proved impossible to control. In 578 the Synod of Auxerre, worried that St Martin's feast was rapidly turning into a pagan orgy (Martin himself was sometimes known as the drunken saint), forbade banqueting on Martinmas Eve.

Yet the celebrations continued; winter had to be properly ushered in. St Martin bonfires were lit in Germany throughout the Middle Ages; and later still the Dutch held Martinmas fire festivals during which boys sang out 'Make fire/Saint Martin comes here'. The phrase is reminiscent of the song to St Bridget at the Celtic February feast of Imbolc (*see* Chapter 2). Having failed to drag the feast of Martinmas into Christian respectability, the Church decided to turn the season to its own account by proclaiming it the time when Church dues and pasture rents had to be paid. That must have helped to dampen the festivities. Martinmas was officially recognised in Anglo-Saxon Law and was first mentioned in the chronicle for the year 913 AD.

That is not the end of St Martin, for he was to become, with St Clement, the patron saint of blacksmiths. The excuse for claiming him for this role was that he was the patron of travellers on horseback and had a horseshoe as his emblem. St Clement, the other patron of the blacksmiths, was a fourth-century martyr who died by being thrown out to sea chained to an anchor. The Woolwich blacksmiths used to carry his image round at the time of his feast day (23 November), and they kept this custom up till the eighteenth century. At Chatham the St Clement's Day feast was celebrated for another hundred years, and at Twyford in Hampshire it went on as long. Up to 1889 a Clem supper was regularly held at the Bugle Inn, and the main toast was always to the blacksmiths. Probably the alteration in the calendar accounts for the confusion between these two saint's days, for St Clement's day was sometimes referred to as Old Martinmas, and some sources give his feast as 4 December.

In ancient times the smiths were a race apart; yet they too had to have a feast to mark the beginning of winter, although it seems to have had nothing to do with the general festival of Samhain. Their craft was looked upon with superstitious awe, and the smith who worked in iron was considered even more of a wizard than the man who could fashion bronze implements. For bronze is a molten alloy which is simply shaped by being poured into clay moulds; iron ore, though it has the advantage of being more generally available, is much harder to work. It has to be beaten into shape at intense heat; and as the smith hammered on his anvil beside a furnace deliberately screened from the sun, people must have watched with fascinated dread as the sparks flew upwards in the gloom. In Celtic settlements the smith's dwelling was at a distance from the rest of the huts, and he was regarded with a mixture of admiration and suspicion. Christianity did nothing to lessen the people's fear. St Patrick prayed to be saved from the 'spells of women and smith and wizards'. To the Saxons he was Wayland Smith, a demi-god of power and cunning, and it has even been suggested that the Yule log was derived from his anvil.[2]

Every feast of fire is also a feast of light. At the Saturnalia the Romans exchanged gifts of candles; and in many All Souls' rituals it is customary to light candles to guide the returning dead. As the solstice approaches and the days get shorter, the need for some sort of artificial light becomes more pressing, and when that was harder to come by people found it important to hold occasional festivals to banish the dark. We find them in every culture from the Hindu Festival of Lights to the Jewish Hanukkah and the Swedish feast of St Lucia.

St Lucia was a Sicilian girl of the third century. She was martyred under Diocletian and, like St Martin, she was adopted by the Church in order to fit in with an existing festival. Her day is celebrated on 13 December, and in Sweden it is known as Little Yule. On that day it is the custom for the youngest girl in the house to get up at 6 am and, dressed in white, take food to her parents and to any animals in the household. This modern custom grew out of the old tradition of choosing a Lucia queen for the whole village. She had to set out before sunrise with a man on horseback, accompanied by a group of maids of honour and by boys representing demons and trolls conquered by the reviving sun.

It comes as rather a surprise to discover that the Church of England's Children's Society has seen fit to take over a pagan feast of light which was first Christianised in Protestant Moravia. The ceremony is centred on an orange pierced by a lighted candle. This pagan symbolism for the light of the sun received a Christian gloss

Christingle Service, Church of England Children's Society

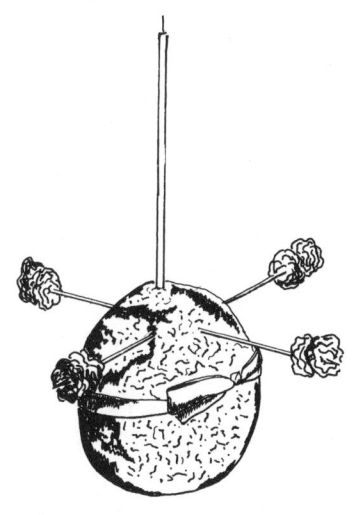

Christingle

Fire and Light ♦ 63

from the Moravians, who gave gifts of oranges (a rare imported fruit) to children who earned them by donations to the poor at Christmas. For them the orange represented the world, the candle the light of the world, and the sweets and nuts with which the fruit was decorated stood for the harvests of the four seasons. The Romans, who also used oranges as part of the feast of Saturnalia, decorated them in a similar manner. For the Moravians, who held a children's service based on these decorated oranges, everything about it was linked to the gifts of God. The orange was called a Christingle. The earliest record of the Christian custom comes from Marienborn in 1747. It is now used as a way of raising money for an Anglican charity, and the children's services based on it can be held at Advent, Christmas or Epiphany, the three seasons at which rituals of fire and light have always been held.

The Jewish festival of Hanukkah was founded by Judah Maccabee and centred on the rededication of the temple for the coming year.[3] It commemorates the original dedication of Solomon's temple, when fire descended from heaven to sanctify the holy place. The festival is one of light, according to Josephus (AD c.37–101), because 'the right to serve God came to the people unexpectedly like a sudden light'; but its importance in the context of a book on winter solstice celebrations throughout Britain comes with its parallel to Christmas. Throughout the diaspora, Jewish communities in Christian countries have made it an alternative festival to Christmas, and transformed it from a temple ceremony to a family holiday accompanied by feasting, card playing (in the face of Rabbinical objections) and the giving of gifts to children. At the same time the original connection with light has been preserved. The special lamps that are lit in each home during this eight-day festival must serve no practical purpose apart from illuminating the reading of the Torah; and no Hanukkah lamp is allowed to be kindled from another but must always be lit from a special source. In every culture this kindling of the ceremonial fires and lights is treated with great reverence.

In Britain the fires of the solstice have been lit since the Bronze Age, although there is little evidence to show what ceremonies went with their kindling. Much has to be left to conjecture, but it is surely possible (as I have suggested in Chapter 1) that the remains of fires, without trace of any cremation, that have been found in the

Hanukkah Festival

centres of the Dartmoor stone circles are evidence of fire rituals.

An ancient but more domestic fire ceremony which persisted until recent centuries took place in the Orkneys. In these northern latitudes, fire was felt to be a protection against the terrors of darkness, when the destructive powers of the trows (described in Chapter 4) are at their height. The most dangerous night of all was said to be 24 December, and at that time the crofters were careful to safeguard their families by performing a simple act of purification involving fire and water. George Mackay Brown tells how 'The mother brought out a basin and filled it with water. The man of the house, priest-like, took three live embers from the fire and dropped them in the water. So, in midwinter, the elements of fire and water were true to the tryst of purification . . . One by one, each member of the family washed himself all over in the fire-kissed water and put on clean clothes.' Then, when all the children had gone to bed, the parents 'made an act of great faith. Though the night outside was thick with trows, they unfastened the door and left the lamp burning.'[4]

Yet despite the obvious piety of the Orkney peasants, who, having observed their ritual, thought it possible that 'Our Lady and

Saint Joseph with their as-yet-hidden treasure would come to their croft that night, seeking shelter',[4] the Church was no happier about the fire ceremonies of the winter solstice than about the pagan bonfires of November. In fact, insofar as the solstice fires were even more closely associated with witch cults, they were that much more threatening to the established religion. One writer has given this account of a mid-winter fire in a present-day coven;[5] 'the priestess or female leader of the coven stands behind a cauldron in which a fire is ignited, while the rest dance round her sunwise with burning torches. They call it the Dance of the Wheel or Yule, and its purpose is "to cause the sun to be reborn". The cauldron here represents the same idea as the "gate", the Great Mother. The fire in it is the Sun-Child in her womb.'

Although fire was used by witches, the burning Yule log, carefully lighted from the embers of its predecessor, was supposed to ward off witches and evil beings, and where it was 'the fiend could do no mischief'.[6] By some sort of homeopathic magic the burning log protected the house against fire and lightning. For this purpose an oak log was especially efficacious, for it was linked to the might of Thor. Even in Cornwall, a Celtic region, which never had much experience of the Norse gods, the Yule log, in this case with the figure of a man roughly chalked on it, was considered a protection against the powers of darkness. In Devon and Somerset, ash takes the place of oak, and the Yule log is transformed into the Ashen or Ashton faggot. It has been described as 'a large bundle of ash logs . . . bound together with branches, willows, brambles or withies. Sometimes chains were used to hold the logs as they could be five feet long and weigh a hundredweight. The bands – nine was the magic number, though there might be as few as four – were watched as they burst open and a secret wish would be made.'[7] This custom is continued to the present day in Somerset, on Christmas Eve at the Luttrell Arms at Dunster and on 5 January (the eve of Old Christmas) at the King William IV at Curry Rivel.

The fires of New Year gave the same protection against the powers of evil as those of the solstice itself. In the middle of the eighth century, Boniface wrote to Pope Zacharius about the pagan Roman rites of the Kalends of January. He explained how the fires of that season were supposed to sanctify the whole house so long as nothing was taken away from them. Like the Orkney embers, the pre-Christian Roman fires of New Year were a family occasion, a blaze that sanctified the hearth. From our Celtic and Norse ancestors we inherit a different type of New Year fire which, like those of Hallowe'en, takes place in the open air. These blazes are often associated with mummers (*see* Chapter 8) or at any rate with people dressed up in strange clothes, who use the occasion for feasting and begging.

So up to the nineteenth century in Allendale, Northumberland, a great bonfire was lit at midnight on New Year's Eve by young men in fancy dress, who then went first footing through the houses. At Burghead on the Moray Firth at Hogmanay (sometimes celebrated at old New Year, 11 January) a tar barrel called a clavie was set on fire by blazing peat and hoisted on a pole known as the spoke. No metal was allowed to be used in this operation, an embargo that reminds us of the suspicion which surrounded the craft of the smith. The 'clavie' was carried round the village, and then rolled down the hillside. As it passed the houses, doors were opened to allow brands to be thrown in for luck, and from these the home fires were lit. When the 'clavie' itself burnt low, its embers were kept as a charm against witchcraft.[8]

That tradition kept two pagan beliefs alive. The first was that of the potency of the New Year fire on the hearth to preserve the home from natural and supernatural dangers. The second is connected with the often repeated theme of rolling a flaming wheel (or circular object such as a barrel) downhill to represent the course of the returning sun.

Such customs were also kept alive in the fires of Epiphany or Twelfth Night, often observed on the old calendar date of 17 January. On the Isle of Man, with its November New Year, the fires of 6 (or 17) January, the last day of Yule, were regarded with the same sort of reverence as were the January New Year fires in other places. These fires had to be purchased. They could not be borrowed or lit from a neighbour's.

On the whole, however, the emphasis at Twelfth Night was on public rather than domestic fires; and although many of them were simply lit as beacons on headlands and high places, others were regarded as having a definite function in increasing the fertility of fields and orchards. In Gloucestershire and Worcestershire, fires lit in the fields on the eve of Twelfth Night were supposed to prevent wheat decay. This may just have had some practical basis in the warming of the soil at that time. The ritual that attended this firelighting, however, must be linked with some faintly remembered practice of sun worship. The farmer and his servants lit twelve small fires and one large one in the cornfield; then, forming themselves into a circle round that fire they let out a great shout which was answered from all the neighbouring farms and villages.

When the Church started to adopt the celebrations of Twelfth Night by celebrating the feast of Epiphany at this season the fire rituals remained. This is particularly so in the east. In the Orthodox church, where Epiphany celebrates Christ's baptism, his first miracle and the feeding of the five thousand as well as the showing forth of the baby at the Temple and the worship of the three kings, the day was called 'This holy day of lights'. The Catholic Church concentrated more on turning the February fires and lights of Bridget's feast of Imbolc into the celebration of Candlemas and the Purification of the Virgin Mary. In doing so they were also taking into account the Roman torchlight processions held at this season in honour of Februa, mother of Mars, which in their turn echoed the myth of Ceres' torchlight search in the underworld for her daughter, Persephone.

Candlemas is also a strictly practical occasion. It is a time when the hours of daylight are beginning to lengthen, and in days when economy was even more necessary than it is now the use of candles could be restricted, especially in poor homes where any form of artificial light was a great luxury and people usually went to bed with the sun. By the laws of the tenth-century King Ethelred, it was at Candlemas that the tax of 'light scot' became due; like the dues of Martinmas, this must have done as much to take the enthusiasm out of any pagan rituals as any purely religious decrees of the Church. Yet the Church itself was concerned to keep this time as a feast of lights. The tapers that were lit in honour of the Purification of the Virgin were so holy that, in common with other sacred flames, and indeed that of the Yule log itself, they had the power to ward off evil spirits, and their wax was a sure antidote to the spells of witchcraft.

The candles which burnt for Mary at this time were reflected in the fires that were kindled for St Bridgit and St Blaize, who had a special power over witches and whose feast day falls on 3 February. It would be good to think that the Church viewed these customs and the pagan rituals they preserved in the same way that George Herbert[9] regarded them in the seventeenth century, 'Light is a great blessing,' he wrote, 'and as great as food for which we give thanks, and those that think this superstitious neither know superstition or themselves.'

In northern latitudes the celebrations of the returning sun in February go back to the time of the Bronze Age stone circle builders. The artist John Glover, whose work on those circles I mentioned in Chapter 1, has noticed that at Castlerigg in Cumbria the alignment which points west towards the setting sun of midsummer carries through eastwards to the rising sun of Candlemas. This is not simply fortuitous, for the Candlemas alignment passes through the tallest stone of the circle.[10]

References:
1. J.G. FRAZER: *The Golden Bough*, Macmillan, 1922
2. A. TILLE: *Yule and Christmas*, D. Nutt, 1899
3. JOHN, x, 22: 'It was the feast of dedication at Jerusalem; it was winter.'
4. GEORGE MACKAY BROWN: *An Orkney Tapestry*, Quartet, 1973
5. W.B. GARDINER: *The Meaning of Witchcraft*, Aquarian Press, 1959
6. JOHN BRAND (1777), quoted by J.G. Frazer in *The Golden Bough*, Macmillan, 1922
7. M. WALKER and HELEN BENNETT: Notes on Somerset Folklore prepared for the Somerset Rural Life Museum
8. CHAMBERS' *Book of Days*, 1886: *Folklore* vii, 1889
9. GEORGE HERBERT: *The Country Parson*, 1675
10. Quoted in *The Ley Hunters' Companion*: PAUL DEVEREUX and IAN THOMSON, Thames & Hudson, 1979

6 ♦ THE PLANTS OF THE SOLSTICE

Barley grain is like seeds of gold.
When you turn a heap with a shovel it flows
With the heavy magic of wealth.
Every grain is a sleeping princess –
Her kingdom is still to come.

TED HUGHES, *Barley*

The winter rituals, traditions and superstitions that are connected with plants, like those centred on fire and light, are all rooted in practical necessity. What matters is the food crop. All the rites connected with vegetation are concerned with it; and the most pertinent are those that are designed to ensure a good corn harvest from one year to the next.

The rituals of the corn start with the aftermath of the harvest and

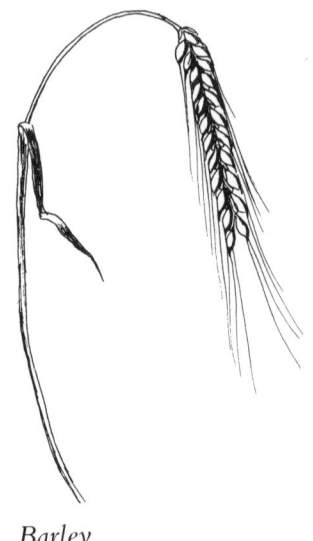

Barley

the preservation of the last sheaf. In many areas this was formed into a corn dolly, whose design varied according to the region. It was kept indoors throughout the winter, and honoured both as a thank offering for the last harvest and a symbol of the seed corn that would provide the next one. This tradition survived until the end of the nineteenth century, and as the design of the dolly varied from district to district so did the customs connected with it. In Staffordshire and Yorkshire the wheat from the last corn sheaf was kept in the kitchen until mid-December, when it was made into a sweet frumenty. This had to be the first food eaten on Christmas morning. In the Lake District, the corn dolly, with a large rosy apple fixed in the middle of it, was hung in the farmer's kitchen until Christmas Day. On that morning the farmer gave the apple to the nicest woman in the house and the corn to the best cow in the byre. The Norsemen, who left more traces of their occupation in that part of the country than in any other, would have felt he was acting

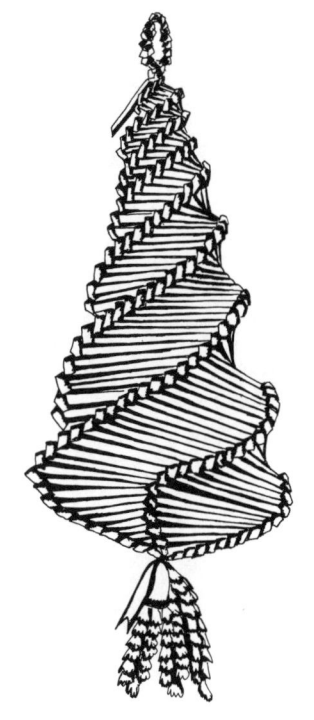

Corn dolly

properly. For Odin, in his aspect as corn spirit, had to be placated with some such rituals – though probably not such a gentle one – to ensure that the fruits of the harvest would stretch throughout the winter.

In some areas the beginning of winter is a time of planting as well as of storing the harvest. In the south-west, Guy Fawkes' Day is still thought to be the best time for planting broad beans. In other areas, St Thomas's Day, 21 December, was considered the proper time, and the belief was that if one bean in the row came up white there would be a death in the family. The idea that broad beans, which have been grown from prehistoric times for their property of regenerating the soil with nitrogen as well as supplementing the cereal crop, are linked with doom probably came about because the Romans used them as part of their funeral rites. Before that, the Celts made a close connection between beans and the supernatural. In some parts of Scotland it was thought that witches rode on beanstalks rather than broomsticks, and in Ireland and Wales 'beanos' or 'bean feasts' were held in honour of the fairies who lived in the haunted barrows. From Suffolk comes the story of the Green Children of Woolpit, who emerged from a hole in the ground and could only be nourished by beans. Their food was a token between the worlds of the natural and the supernatural, the living and the dead; and it was as such that beans had their place in the Samhain festivities.

Hazel

The hazel has similar attributes. In Ireland its nuts made up part of the tribute which men were expected to pay to the fairies at this time. In other Celtic areas the link between the hazel and Samhain continued to within living memory. One writer tells of 'a hazel grove beside a wishing well in the Isle of Skye, where the children used to gather nuts just before Hallowe'en'.[1] For the Celts, the hazel was a magical tree, partly because its flexible branches were used in water divining but mostly because the plant was supposed to have the power to protect people from both the supernatural forces of witchcraft and the natural disasters of fire and flood. Although scholars point out that the 'witch' in 'witch hazel' is derived from the Anglo-Saxon *wicen*, to bend, there is no such simple explanation of the German term for the hazel *Zauberstrauch*, the magic tree.

The plant which we now associate most strongly with Hallowe'en customs is the apple. This is the fruit which has long been held as a talisman between men and gods. According to Druidic rites, the immortal souls had to pass through water in order to reach Avalon, the apple land and country of the immortals. That belief has dwindled now to the game of ducking for apples in buckets of water. Hallowe'en apples are also used for divination. In one simple form, the letter which the pared peel most resembles is the initial of the enquirer's future mate. Sometimes, as is the case with the Allan apples of Cornwall, simply eating them at Hallowe'en will bring good luck.[2] Apples have always been associated with ordeals by fire, though the only relic of this is the rather dangerous game which requires the players to eat an apple balanced on a small rod of wood which also supports a lighted candle.

The apple becomes important again around Twelfth Night, when ceremonies are performed to ensure that the orchard will bear well in the coming year. At the end of the last century, the parishioners in some parts of East Cornwall used 'to walk in procession visiting the principal orchards in the parish. One tree in each orchard was selected to be the representative of the rest, it was saluted and sprinkled with cider to ensure a fruitful crop in the coming year.'[2]

In Somerset, apple wassailing (encouraged by the local cider companies) still takes place on Twelfth Night, or more usually on old Twelfth Night (17 January). One custom in that county was to put a piece of bread soaked in cider on the branches of the chosen

Leafless apple tree

tree. In other places it was simply enough to observe how the sun shone on Christmas morning. If it sent its rays through the apple trees, it was a sign that the next year's crop would be a good one.

All these plants are edible, but the evergreens which have been brought indoors to decorate the solstice celebrations at least from the time that the Romans were here, and probably much earlier, cannot be eaten, and among them only rosemary and bay can be used for flavouring. The obvious symbolism of the evergreen plants is the perennial fertility of nature. The need to be assured of this at a time when most trees are leafless has always been so strong that the Church quickly had to succumb to the pagan practice of using evergreens as part of the solstice festivities; although it did do its best to put an end to the practice. In AD 575 the Chapter of Bishop Martin of Bracea made it unlawful for the faithful to observe 'the heathen festivals and to adorn their houses with laurels and green trees'. This prohibition seems to have been more or less effective until the twelfth century; but by the fifteenth evergreens were so much a part of the Christmas celebrations that it was expected that 'everymans house, as also parish Churches, were decked with Holme, Ivy, Bayes and whatsoever the season of the yeare aforded to be greene'.[3] The same writer records that on 1 February 1444 a storm tore up a tree in Cornhill, which was still 'nayled full of Holme and Ivy, for disport of Christmas'.

Although the Puritans did their best to put an end to the use of Christmas evergreens the tradition persisted. One seventeenth-century writer observed that 'It is not very long since the custome of setting up garlands in churches hath been left off with us: and in some places setting up of holly, ivy, rosemary, bayes, yew etc. in Churches at Christmas is still in use'.[4] By the beginning of the eighteenth century the use of evergreens was fully reinstated. John Gay wrote:

> When rosemary and bays, the poet's crown,
> Are bawled in frequent cries throughout the town,
> Then judge the festival of Christmas near –
> Christmas the joyous period of the year.
> Now with bright holly all the temples strow,
> With laurel green and sacred mistletoe.[5]

As Gay hints, however, in the Church's despite, the winter evergreens retained their pagan associations. They were used for divination, especially at the feast of St Thomas (21 December) which fell near the true solstice. In some parts of the country an unmarried girl placed a sprig under her pillow at that time, and then prayed to dream of her future husband. Everywhere St Thomas's Day was an excuse for 'gooding', a form of begging for Christmas fare in return for some token or gift. *The Gentleman's Magazine* for April 1794 records the St Thomas custom whereby women took sprigs of evergreen to the people who had helped them in the past year, and from whom, presumably, they looked for further help during the winter.

Although evergreens of all sort are a natural symbol of the persistence of vegetable life through the dark, dead days of the year, they each have their own particular characteristics. I will start with the holly, the most widely accepted Christmas decoration of them all, and one that has been so since the Middle Ages. In the fourteenth-century romance of Sir Gawain the Green Knight rides into Arthur's feast carrying an axe and a holly bough.

Many superstitions are associated with the traditional use of holly at the solstice. It used to be thought unlucky to bring holly into the house before Christmas Eve, or to have it there after Twelfth Night, for after that date every leaf and sprig of berries would turn into a mischievous spirit. However, holly that had been used for

Holly

church decorations brought good health to the beasts if it were hung in the cowsheds; and cattle and sheep would thrive if they saw holly on Christmas Eve. Holly was also used for divination. In one custom tiny pieces of candle were put on the holly leaves. These were then placed in a tub of water to float. If they remained buoyant the projects they represented were sure to prosper.

As holly was always thought of as a male plant, it was never used as part of the St Catherine decorations of 25 November, for that saint was the protector of young unmarried girls. On the other hand, the clinging ivy is female, and is particularly relevant to Christmas as the berries ripen after the winter solstice. Its part in divination came at New Year. A leaf put under a bowl of water at that time promised a happy twelve months ahead if it was still green and fresh at Twelfth Night. Like the holly, the ivy was a plant that afforded protection against witchcraft.

We do not think of rosemary as one of the indispensable Christmas evergreens, but in the early Middle Ages it had an important place in Christian mythology. The herb was supposed to grow to the height that Christ attained as a man. When it reached that stature it could only increase in breadth, never in height. It was thought only to thrive in the gardens of the just. Its flowers are supposed to appear at Twelfth Night and, according to a Spanish legend, they owe their colour to the blue grey of the Virgin's cloak, which she threw over a rosemary bush. Before that happened the rosemary flower was white.

The evergreens that decorated the Roman Saturnalia, such as the bay leaves, sacred to Apollo, the victor's laurel and the juniper potent against all sorts of black magic, have never become part of our Christmas tradition. In Scotland, however, the protective powers of juniper were felt to be so potent at New Year that, well into

Ivy

Rosemary

Juniper

the Christian era, branches of the shrub were burnt to protect both men and cattle.

Only the mistletoe, the sacred plant of the Druids and of even earlier priesthoods, has never been completely accepted by Christianity. In only a very few cases, such as a carving on a tomb in Bristol cathedral, does the plant or its image make its way inside a Christian building. The eighteenth-century antiquarian William Stukeley wrote of its introduction to York cathedral on Christmas Eve as a deliberate throwback to the Druids, who, as he believed, celebrated the solstice by placing mistletoe on their altars. 'The custom is still preserved in the North,' he wrote, 'and was lately at York: on the eve of Christmas-Day they carry Misletoe to the high Altar of the Cathedral and proclaim a public and universal liberty, pardon, and freedom to all sorts of inferior and even wicked people at the gates of the city, towards the four quarters of Heaven.'[6] As a rule, however, the church could not tolerate the strong pagan implications of the plant and frowned on its use as a decoration in a Christian place, although people always insisted on taking some into their own homes.

The plant is common enough. Anywhere in the country you can see it at any time of the year, particularly growing on apple trees, poplar, elm and lime. There is even a flourishing colony of it by the side of the M4 just west of Heathrow. To the ancients it was the mistletoe growing on the oak, Thor's tree, that was particularly sacred, and for some reason this is harder to find. Two explanations are given for the potency of mistletoe as a religious symbol and as an all-heal herb. One is that it remains green when its host plant has shed its leaves for the winter; the other is that it grows midway between earth and heaven, with no roots in the soil, and so was thought to be of a divine nature. For the Druids it was the chief plant of both the winter and the summer solstices. In winter the ceremonial cutting of the plant took place on the sixth day of the full moon nearest to the New Year. It was long thought to be a specific against witchcraft, and up to the seventeenth century people wore a sprig round their necks as a talisman. Its role as the kissing bough in our Christmas celebrations, presumably derives from the belief that the plant has aphrodisiac properties. The modern custom dates back at least to the fifteenth century. Erasmus (1466–1536) recorded a tradition of kissing under a dome of mistletoe bound up with red ribbons, ivy and yew.

 The Christmas tree, the decorated fir which forms the centrepiece of Christmas for so many people, is, as everyone knows, a Victorian introduction to this country, a custom brought over from Germany by Prince Albert. Yet it has a much earlier origin. Tradition has it that in the eighth century St Boniface dedicated the evergreen fir tree to the Holy Child as a counter to the sacred oak of Odin. At least one writer took a contrary view. A contributor to Willis's *Current Notes* for February 1854 claimed that the idea of the Christmas tree came from Egypt. He dogmatically declared that 'The Christmas-tree is from Egypt, and its origin dates from a period long antecedent to the Christian era. The palm-tree is known to put forth a shoot every month, and a spray of this tree, with twelve shoots on it, was used in Egypt, at the time of the winter solstice, as a symbol of the year completed.'

 Two other views on the origin of the Christmas tree both come from Germany. According to one of them it evolved from the Paradise Tree, a fir tree decorated with apples and ringed by candles which was the central object of the German medieval mystery plays. The other source claims that the Christmas tree grew from Martin Luther's spontaneous decision, when he saw stars shining through a fir tree, to decorate one in like manner for his young son.

 Willis's contributor was right, however, in claiming that the place of trees at the winter solstice goes well back into the pre-Christian era. According to one authority,[7] the Celts felled a ritual tree at this time and then buried it, presumably as a symbol of the death of vegetation. In much the same way as the Church uses the

Christmas tree (in some instances even connecting it with the Cross), the Romans honoured the myth of the death and revival of Adonis by paying homage to a pine tree, whose cone was the symbol of immortality. Perhaps it was rituals such as these which inspired the old country belief, recorded by the late nineteenth-century writer Richard Jefferies, that certain trees ought only to be felled on 31 December and 1 January. The practical reason was that in mid-winter the sap would have withdrawn so that the felled timber would last longer.

Then there are the flowers of Christmas. In these days of hot-house plants and forced early bulbs, it is hard to imagine a flowerless time, when the black hellebore or Christmas rose (the flower of St Agnes as it was sometimes called) was the only plant to bloom. No wonder this waxy flower was thought to have the power to drive away demons and dispel melancholy; nor that, according to Gerard's *Herbal*, it was good 'for all those that are troubled with black choler'.

Christmas rose

Yet there is one flowering plant, the Glastonbury Thorn, that is particularly renowned for its solstice blossoms. There are three specimens of this early flowering hawthorn (*Crataegus praecox*) in modern Glastonbury. One stands in front of the parish Church, another in the grounds of the ruined abbey and a third on the slope of Weary-all Hill on the outskirts of the town. This last one grows on the site of the original thorn, which was supposed to have been miraculously planted there by Joseph of Arimathea. The story went that St Joseph, on a mission to bring Christianity to Britain, reached the Isle of Avalon after a weary journey across the inland seas of

Somerset. He struck his staff into the hillside and, although it was winter, the dead wood immediately burst into flower. Every year after that it was supposed to blossom at the time of Christ's nativity. Frequently the three thorns of Glastonbury still do flower (or at any rate come into full leaf) on Christmas Day (or on old Christmas Day, 6 January).

Cuttings from the Glastonbury thorns have been grafted onto hawthorns throughout the country, and in the mild west country

Glastonbury Thorn

particularly there have been records of their winter flowering. Several reports show that many people believed that the true date of Christmas should be reckoned by the day the hawthorn flowered. In the eighteenth century, when the thorn at Quainton in Buckinghamshire did not flower on Christmas Day, the people insisted on waiting eleven days in order to celebrate Christmas according to the old calendar.[7]

The nineteenth-century diarist and country vicar Francis Kilvert had no doubt that old Christmas was the right time to see the thorn in bloom. Accordingly he went early in January 1878 to the Rad-

The Plants of the Solstice ♦ 81

norshire village of Dolfach to see the wonder. He found 'Fifteen people watching round the tree to see it blow at midnight.' His host's daughter gave him a spray of the thorn to put 'in soft water'. She made a habit of gathering a sprig at midnight on each old Christmas Eve and keeping it by her all year.[8]

Up to the reign of Charles I, a branch of the flowering Glastonbury thorn was sent to the ruling monarch each Christmas. This superstitious practice so infuriated one no-nonsense Somerset Puritan that he tried to cut the thorn bush down. Tradition has it that he got a splinter in his eye for his pains, and the thorn remained standing. Not for long though. Cromwell's orders were more effective, the tree was cut down to a stump. The one that now grows on Weary-all Hill stands with a stone slab at its base.

Although the Glastonbury thorn is so grounded in Christian folklore, there is another pre-Christian explanation for the mysterious blossoming of this bush. It is based on the assumption that the thorns of Herefordshire and the Welsh borders are not cuttings from Glastonbury but exist in their own right. According to this theory[9] they were all planted by an immigrant Celtic tribe for whom the early blossoming hawthorn was a sacred totem. This tribe is supposed to have come up the Bristol Channel and diverged at the mouth of the Avon, some of the families going west across the Somerset lakes and some north along the course of the Wye.

Those that went north seem to have given special significance to the blackthorn, which has been revered in this region for centuries. In Christian times it was said to be the tree from which the crown of thorns was made and, like the Glastonbury thorn, it bloomed on old Christmas Eve. At New Year small branches of it were woven into a sphere, perhaps in representation of a crown. This was passed quickly over a straw fire, while the words 'Old Cider' were chanted over it. Finally it was taken into the house to be added to the other Christmas decorations.[10]

The Celtic Isle of Man has its own solstice bloom. This is the myrrh or Sweet Cicely which, although less reliable than the Glastonbury Thorn, is looked on to blossom on Christmas Eve or on the eve of Old Christmas Day. They say it flowers for the space of one hour. The only record I have found of it doing so relates to the year 1890.[11]

For most people the first flower of the year is the snowdrop. The

Druids planted them in great numbers in their groves, and you will still see large colonies of them in places that appear to have been prehistoric sacred sites. I think especially of those that grow (sometimes to quite a size) in the round Celtic churchyards of Wales, and the great masses around Cave Gate in Hertfordshire (*see* Chapter 3).

Snowdrop

Our ancestors did not simply find snowdrops beautiful to look at as an early promise of spring. They had a practical use for them. Their bulbs were made into balm to cure all manner of winter ailments, and they were thought to be especially efficacious in the case of chilblains. Yet the white snowdrops had a dreadful aspect. As they flower at a time when many old and frail people are succumbing to the rigours of winter, they were reminiscent of the pallor of death. So in many areas it was thought unlucky to bring them into the house, and many a February death was blamed on the flower. On the other hand, snowdrops were also held to be symbols of purity, and as Candlemas bells they were dedicated to the Virgin Mary on 2 February.

The yellow aconite, introduced into England from the Swiss Alps, from which many Celtic tribes originated, is another plant that was both feared and blessed. Although it was given as part of the New Year gifts in Lincolnshire, and although it was believed to have power against the sting of scorpions, its juice was so deadly to man and beast that it earned the name of Thora (poison), Wolfes-

Winter Aconite

bane and Sagittarius. This last came about because its venom was used on arrow heads. More fancifully, a substance made from these juices was known as 'the flying ointment'; for witches were supposed to smear their bodies with it before they took to the air.

The other yellow flower of winter, the crocus, takes us back to November and All Hallows, for it supplied the saffron that was supposed to represent the fires of Purgatory. As such it was used in cakes to be eaten on All Souls' Day. That custom was kept up until the eighteenth century, although in some areas, and particularly in the lace-making town of Olney in Buckinghamshire the saffron cakes were eaten on 25 November. That is St Catherine's Day and, in her role as patron of lace-makers, she undertook to find husbands for unmarried girls.

Of a much wider significance is the way the rituals surrounding the plants at New Year link with those of November and the storing of the harvest. For many centuries the twelve days of Christmas were the only holiday the farm labourers could rely on, and immediately they were over the ploughing for the following year's crop began. So traditionally the first Monday after Twelfth Night is known as Plough Monday. For many it was a feast day, originating perhaps in the Roman festival of Compitalia which celebrated the January ploughing. In Britain up to the nineteenth century it was kept in a variety of ways, sometimes by the performance of special mummers' plays, which I shall describe in Chapter 8. In Norfolk, where the day was known as Plowlich Day, the festivities were more simple. According to Blomefield, 'There was a light in many churches called the plow light, maintained by old and young persons who were husbandmen, before some image; who on Plough Monday had a feast and went about with a plough, and some dances to support it'.[12]

Much the same sort of thing went on in Essex. The accounts at Heybridge near Malden read, 'Item: received of the gadrynge of the White Plow £0.11.3d'. Beside that entry there is a note. 'Q: Does this mean Plough Monday: on which the Country People come and dance and make a gathering as on May Day.'[13]

The leaping dances were supposed to represent the height to which the new corn would grow, so the most athletic of the young men were chosen to perform them. In many parts of the country one other rite was performed on Plough Monday to ensure the success of the new harvest. The corn dolly that had been kept safely indoors all winter was ceremonially buried in the first furrow.

An evergreen marks the last plant ritual of winter. In many places a bough of box was hung in the churches at Candlemas to replace the Christmas decorations. It stayed there till Easter.

Box

References:
1. F. MARIAN MCNEILL: *Hallowe'en*, Albyn Press, 1970
2. MARGARET COURTENAY and T. QUILLER COUCH: *East Cornwall Christmas Customs*, 1883
3. JOHN STOW: *The Survey of London*, published in 1618, written 1598
4. W. COLES: *The Art of Simpling*, 1656
5. JOHN GAY: *Trivia*, 1713
6. WILLIAM STUKELEY: *The Medalic History of M.A.V. Carausius*, 1757–9, Book II, pp. 163–4

7. *Gentleman's Magazine*, 1753
8. *Kilvert's Diary* edited by William Plomer, Cape 1973 (abridged) and 1976
9. VAUGHAN CORNISH: *Historic Thorn Trees in the British Isles*, n.d.
10. ETHEL URLIN: *Festivals and Saints Days*, Simpkin Marshall, 1915
11. A.W. MOORE: *The Folklore of the Isle of Man*, Brown & Son, Douglas, 1891
12. BLOMEFIELD'S *Norfolk*, Vol IV, p.287
13. W. CAREW HAZLITT: *Popular Antiquities of Great Britain*, Vol 1, 1870, from material collected by John Brand in the eighteenth century

7 ♦ THE ANIMALS OF THE SOLSTICE

> Christmas Eve and twelve of the clock,
>   'Now they are all on their knees,'
> An elder said as we sat in a flock
>   By the embers in hearthside ease.
>
> We pictured the meek mild creatures where
>   They dwelt in their strawy pen,
> Nor did it occur to one of us there
>   To doubt they were kneeling then.
>
> THOMAS HARDY, *The Oxen*

This tradition that the cattle kneel on Christmas Eve is part of a long-established convention that puts the ox and the ass beside the manger where the infant Christ lay. The idea of the kneeling animals was particularly appealing to country people, and reports of their doing so and of the powers of speech that were given to the creatures on this one night of the year come from all over England. Hardy's poems were rooted in the folk beliefs of Wessex, but the same tradition lived farther north. In his diary, Francis Kilvert[1] made a note of what James Weston, an old Herefordshire man, told him about the beasts kneeling at Staunton-on-Wye. 'I was watching them on Old Christmas Eve,' the old man said, 'and at 12 o'clock the oxen that were standing knelt down upon their knees and there they stayed kneeling and moaning, the tears running down their faces.'

A slightly earlier story comes from Cornwall, where John Brand (the eighteenth-century collector of folklore) was told 'by an honest countryman living on the edge of St Stephen's Down near Launceston' that, about twelve o'clock on Christmas night, the two oldest oxen fell on their knees and made 'a cruel moan like Christian creatures'.[2] Similar reports, with a slight elaboration, come from the Isle of Man, for the Manxmen believe that only bullocks of seven years old or more are moved to fall on their knees on Christmas night.

The tradition of the kneeling animals is still not completely dead.

I have met country people, now in middle age, who remember being told the story by half-believing parents, who like Hardy wished it could be true. A verse of a Somerset carol collected by R.L. Tongue about 1940 is based on the belief that it happened. It runs:

> At Chrissimass, at Chrissimass
> Long time ago
> Ox and ass they curchied down
> All in the snow.[3]

Some versions of the story give the kneeling animals the power of speech although I have found no record of the words they are meant to have uttered. Perhaps this gentle pice of folklore grew out of one of the nativity plays performed in the Middle Ages and influenced by St Francis, who is said to have used real animals to illustrate the story of Christ's birth.

The part that the animals played in the pre-Christian rituals of the winter solstice was far less mild. The animal rites and sacrifices of this season are of very ancient origin, and in many forms they bring together the needs of both pastoral and arable cultures. J.G. Frazer[4] has described the way in which animals in many parts of Europe were identified with the corn spirit and with the death and resurrection of the gods of vegetation. That belief persisted into the Christian era; and the same farmers who hoped their beasts might be kneeling on Christmas Eve also hoped to prevent bad luck in the coming year by giving them extra fodder on Christmas Day. In giving way to that superstition they were acting on the pagan belief that the corn was mysteriously linked to the beasts who ate it, and that this ritual feed would cause both animals and fields to flourish.

Yet for thousands of years the real assurance of continued good fortune came from the proper sacrifice to the gods, including Jehovah himself. This always arose from the need to cull the herds at the beginning of winter. We have archaeological evidence that it happened in the Neolithic era (*see* Chapter 2) and written records that it was carried on, through the ceremonies of the Celtic Samhain and the November slaughtering of the Anglo-Saxon *blot monath*, to the Smithfield of nineteenth-century London. In 1871 a contributor to *The Gentleman's Magazine* wrote of the cattle show week: 'Your regular town man makes a pilgrimage as regularly to Islington as he

The Smithfield Cattle Show, Agricultural Hall, Islington, 1871

does to the Derby or the pantomime.' The 'regular town man' would probably have been hard put to explain his fascination with the penned beasts, but it probably owed a lot to the ancient belief that the death of cattle is an integral part of the beginning of winter.

For our culture, the element of sacrifice in this slaughter had its origin in the bull cult of Northern Syria, which flourished around 4000 BC. From those ceremonies came the rituals associated with Tarvos, the bull deity of Crete, who represented the sun, and the Mithraic rites of mid-winter. In Britain they survived to the nineteenth century in such customs and traditions as the Advent Sunday bull baiting at St Madron's near Penzance and the mumming figures of the Wiltshire Christmas bull and the Dorset 'Ooser'. The Wiltshire figure was a creation with bottle eyes, large horns and a lolling tongue; the 'Ooser' was a man in a bull's mask who attended the Christmas revels. The headpiece he wore was described as a 'wooden mask of large size, features grotesquely human, long flowing locks and a pair of bullock horns projecting right and left of the forehead'.[5] Another man in a bull's mask was Old Bronzen Face, who took part in the Black Godiva festival at Southam near Coventry;[6] he was more sinister than the others, and more representative of the horned god of the witches.

The Animals of the Solstice ♦ 89

Dorset Ooser

All these grotesques, no matter how they were fashioned or received, embodied the link between the cult of the bull and the fertility of the land. The sacred animal, who had to die at this time, was partner to the earth or the Great Mother, just as Zeus in the shape of a bull captured Europa. In the most ancient myths, such as those included in the Gilgamesh epic of Mesopotamia, the bull is deified as the weather god, an aspect of the creature's control over the fortunes of agriculture. There is plenty of evidence to show that it was the real animal and not some abstract emblem that was so venerated. The extent of the animal's significance to prehistoric peoples can be judged from the evidence of the ox burials discovered by O.G.S. Crawford beside the megalithic tombs at Lough Gur near the Boyne and at Bryn Celli Dhu in Anglesey.

As the bull generally represented the sun, so the cow stood for the moon. In *The White Goddess* Robert Graves gave her a central part in the mid-winter mysteries, for it was in cow's form that Isis circled the coffin of the vegetable god Osiris, going round it seven times to symbolise the seven lunar months leading up to the solstice. Frazer showed that the corn spirit could occasionally take the form of a cow as well as that of an ox or bull, although it was mostly represented by the latter. Dionysius, as a god of vegetation, took the form of either a bull or a goat; and the sacramental food (often in the form of the last sheaf of the previous harvest) that was given to the animals at the solstice in historic times was shared among all the beasts in the byre. In Scotland when the last sheaf or corn dolly was mixed with the animals' feed on the morning of Yule, the cows and calves were given precedence.

As a horned beast, the bull of ritual and mythology is sometimes classified with the stag, the traditional quarry of the hunter. In North America, the hunted deer became associated with the kneeling oxen of Christmas Eve after the missionaries had done their work among the Indians. In his *Sketches of Upper Canada*, Howison recalls meeting an Indian at midnight on Christmas Eve who beckoned him to silence and said, 'Me watch to see the deer kneel; this is Christmas night, and all the deer fall upon their knees to the Great Spirit and look up.'[7]

In our traditions, it is the reindeer, an animal that is hunted like the stag, used for milk like a dairy cow and can be ridden or used for draught like a horse, that is the central creature of the solstice festivities. The link between the reindeer and Sleipnir, Odin's eight-footed horse, was discussed in Chapter 4, but its origin as a sacred winter beast goes much farther back than Norse mythology. At Stellmoor, a Neolithic site near Hamburg, the bodies of twelve reindeer were found on the floor of the lake together with a pole which once stood on the shore surmounted by a reindeer skull, whose flesh was presumably eaten at some ritual meal and whose brain, it is believed, was offered to the gods. There is no way of knowing at what time of year these sacrifices to propitiate the god of the hunters took place, nor the form of the ceremonies that accompanied them. Two suggestions have been put forward. According to one, the bodies were drowned as part of the sacrificial rites of midsummer. The other theory is that the beasts represented an offering to the gods to ensure the winter's food supply, some of the reindeer meat actually being preserved in the ice of the lake. At whatever season it happened, it is certain that the deaths of the reindeer took place as part of a religious ceremony. In the early

Kentish hodening horse

1940s, a polished bone with a perforated base was found on the site. This acts as a 'bull roarer' when it is swung in an anti-clockwise direction. The sound that similar crude instruments give out, when they are used in the initiation rites of primitive people throughout the world, is thought to represent the voice of the god.[8]

Yet in most countries of north-west Europe it is the horse rather than any form of horned beast who was yoked to the chariot of the sun, and whose sacrifice was central to the winter rites of Odin and Freyr. The spirit of the horse represented the sky god to whom the flesh of the real animal was sacrificially offered. In recent centuries, the horse sacrifice has been symbolised by various winter processions in which a horse's skull (or at least its jaw) mounted upon a pole formed the focal point. Such a procession was a regular Christmas event at Ramsgate in Kent up to the end of the last century. This Kentish 'hodening' horse, with a string attached to its lower jaw, was the equivalent of the Welsh *mari-lwyd*, the horse skull that was carried round from house to house at New Year.

Archaeological evidence has shown that the horse was domesticated, and presumably sacrificed, from Neolithic times. At that stage it was no majestic beast that was offered to the gods but a creature resembling the true and now nearly extinct 12-hand, dun coloured Exmoor pony, with its characteristic mottled muzzle. That tiny horse was transformed by the imaginative power of the

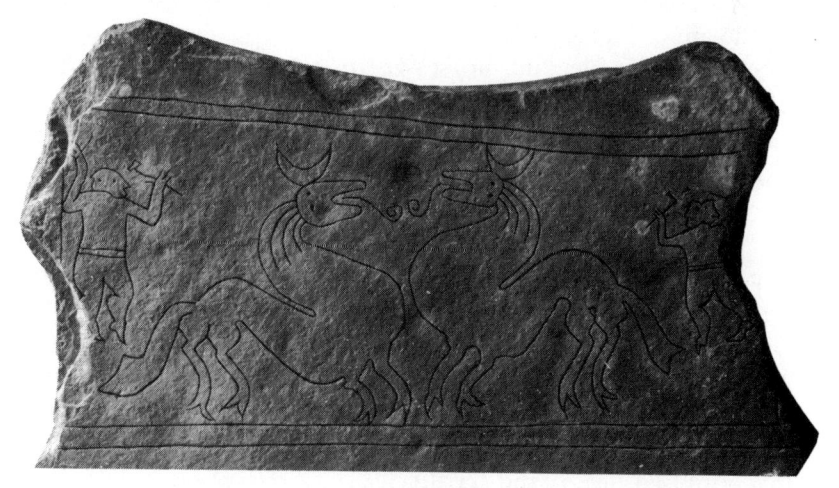

Häggeby Stone, Uppland, Sweden

The Animals of the Solstice ♦ 93

solstice rituals into a fabulous animal of a speed, strength and beauty unknown to any real quadruped. There is even evidence that actual horses were made to feed this illusion by having antlers strapped to their heads to give them the qualities of the stag and the sacred bull. Dr Hilda Davidson[9] refers to the Haggeby stone at Uppland in Sweden which shows a fight between two horses who have horns in the shape of crescent moons on their heads. To the irreverent that is a little reminiscent of the Reverend Sydney Smith's prank of fixing antlers to a couple of donkeys at Combe Fleury (his Quantock parish) in response to a local lady who had declared that the vicarage grounds would be improved by being transformed into a deer park.

Sydney Smith's donkeys were absurd, but the importance of the horse in maintaining the agriculture on which most of his early nineteenth-century contemporaries depended was such that the real beast, unembellished by horns, was still subject to some of the winter ceremonies that surrounded the pagan horse sacrifices. The most puzzling of these is the centuries-long English tradition of bleeding horses for the good of their health on Boxing Day. I cannot tell whether that represented a token sacrifice, whether it arose out of a confusion between St Stephen the first martyr (whose day falls on 26 December) and Stephen the early Scandinavian evangelist (who as a horseman became the protector of sick horses), or whether it was simply a date that fitted in most conveniently with the annual farm holiday.

The custom of bleeding horses at this time is supposed to have been introduced into Britain by the Danes. By the sixteenth century it had become an established practice of good husbandry, and Thomas Tusser the writer of some homely English *Georgics* declared in prose: 'About Christmas is a very proper time to bleed Horses in, for then they are commonly at house, then Spring comes on, the Sun being now come back from the winter solstice, and there are three or four days of rest, and if it be upon St Stephen's Day, it is not the worse, seeing that there are with it three days of rest or at least two.' Horses, like horned cattle, were often identified with the corn spirit and this was especially true of mares. With their foals they were often given the last sheaf of the harvest to ensure their continued health and fertility.

Frazer also shows that, in a somewhat different way, the same identification between animals and the gods of vegetation held true for the boar. Once again this did not always apply strictly to the actual animal. The Baltic 'Christmas Boar', for example, was a cake baked from the first rye of harvest. It was mixed with salt and used as cattle feed at New Year and Epiphany. In Scandinavia the cake was actually baked in the shape of a pig and given to the ploughmen and the plough oxen to eat at the time of the first ploughing. The cake took the place of the real boar that was once sacrificed at Yule in a ceremony performed by priests and tribal chiefs. In Christian times, when that ritual together with all the other solemn rites of the harvest had degenerated into superstitious customs, the practices were usually carried out by yeoman farmers.

It was left to the young, the poor and the disestablished to take part in the customs that were concerned with small, wild animals rather than the farmyard beasts. In England the practice of hunting small animals as part of a winter ceremony went on well into the eighteenth century. Up to that date the landowners of Suffolk, Kent and Sussex gave a general freedom to the common people to hunt game and squirrels on private property throughout St Andrew's Day (30 November). In the eighteenth century, the squirrel hunt in the Kent parish of Eashing was described as a yearly diversion 'when the labourers and lower kind of people assembling together, form a lawless rabble, and being accoutred with guns, poles, clubs and other such weapons, spend the greatest part of the day in parading through the woods and grounds, with loud shoutings and under the pretence of demolishing the squirrels, some few of which they kill, they destroy numbers of hares, pheasants, partridges, and in short whatever comes their way, breaking down the hedges and doing much mischief, and in the evening betaking themselves to the alehouse finish their career there in drunkenness, as is usual with such sort of gentry.'[10]

Much more mysterious than this riotous method of ridding the landlord of pests while making petty contributions to the peasants' larders is the ritual hunting of the wren. That can never have served any practical purpose, although it was often made an excuse for begging. On the Isle of Man, where the custom persisted longer and in a more elaborate form than in most other parts of Britain, the wren hunt took place either on Christmas afternoon or St Stephen's Day. An eighteenth-century writer described what happened: 'On

Hunting the Wren, Ramsey, Isle of Man

the 24th of December, towards evening, all the servants in general have a holiday, they go not to bed all night, but ramble about till the bells ring in all the Churches, which is at 12 o'clock; prayer being over they go to hunt the wren, and after having found one of these poor birds, they kill her, and lay her on a bier with the utmost solemnity, bringing her to the parish church, and burying her with a whimsical kind of solemnity, singing dirges over her in the Manx language, which they call her knell, after which Christmas begins.'[11]

Another writer[12] believed that the custom was founded on the story of a beautiful fairy who seduced men to follow her to the sea, where they perished. She had the power to change into a wren, and

Wren

so escaped death from a knight who had vowed to kill her and save the land from her ravages. She escaped, but every New Year's Day she had to become a wren and perish by human hands. This story gave rise to the superstition that wren feathers collected at the turn of the year gave twelve months' protection against shipwreck. In Cornwall, the hunting of the wren on St Stephen's Day was said to have its origin in the legend that, just as the saint was about to escape from his prison cell, a wren alerted the gaolers.

It is a Christian notion that the wren is an evil creature; for the early Church feared the power of this small bird because it had been sacred to the Druids, in just the same way that it shunned the pagan power of mistletoe. The question remains as to why this rather dowdy little creature should ever have been found so potent. The brothers Grimm collected one story which could explain why it became the Celtic king of the birds and was so closely connected with the rites of the solstice. According to this, the wren is the bird which got nearest to the sun, and it did so by hiding in the eagle's feathers when that bird soared to its greatest height. As a general rule, the wren enjoyed a special protection, for it was thought to be extremely unlucky to kill one or to harm its nest. So the ritual slaughter of the wren at Christmas could be considered part of the general reversal of the order of things that characterised the Saturnalia.

One other suggestion has been put forward. The wren was once generally referred to as a troglodyte, from the erroneous supposition that it built its nest 'in the form of a cavern, with one very small and narrow aperture, through which the birds gain an entrance'.[13] But the nineteenth-century ornithologist hastened to add, 'It does not appear that the wren's nest is narrower or more cavern-like than that of other small birds.' A more likely explanation is given by Ralph Whitlock,[14] who feels it likely that 'the wren became associated with the ideas of the Underworld because of its habit of creeping into crevices of rocks and caves and perhaps of tombs constructed with great stones. As such it could logically be identified with the powers of darkness which at the time of the winter solstice appear to threaten all life and vegetation.'

Whatever its origins, the wren hunt like many other winter rites always concluded, in recent centuries at least, with a noisy procession in which the participants begged food and money for the solstice celebrations. In the case of the wren hunting the lucky feathers were sold as an indirect form of begging. In a few scattered areas the custom still persists though some inanimate object is usually substituted for the bird. One English writer, while living in Connemarra, discovered a boy who took round a potato in a jar in place of the wren.[15]

Strangely, considering they were by tradition present when Mithras emerged from a cleft in the rocks and when Christ was born in a cave, there are few rituals connected with sheep at the time of the winter solstice. Perhaps this is partly because goats and sheep may have been considered together as one species. Certainly primitive breeds of sheep are so goat-like that before the Middle Ages it must have been quite hard to distinguish the one from the other. The only winter ritual I have discovered that is definitely connected with sheep concerns a strip of skin taken from the breast of the animal killed at Christmas or New Year. In Scotland, at Hogmanay, the participants of this ritual walked sunwise round the fire, passing the skin flaming like a torch from hand to hand. Each person had to make the sign of the cross as they held the strip and then to wave it three times over their head in a sunwise direction. It was a sign of sure misfortune to anyone holding the strip if its fire was extinguished as he performed these gestures.[16]

It is an almost inexplicable custom. It seems to be a mixture of Christian and pagan superstition, and may have some connection with the Roman February fertility rites, which made use of strips of skin from the sacrificial goats. Certainly in the Celtic calendar sheep were the most important creatures of that month. The feast of Imbolc, with which it begins, was largely a celebration of the start of the lambing season and the lactation of the ewes.

References:
1. *Francis Kilvert's Diary*, 5 January 1878, edited by William Plomer, Cape, 1973 (abridged) and 1976
2. W. CAREW HAZLITT: *Popular Antiquities of Great Britain*, Vol I, 1879, edited from material collected by John Brand in the eighteenth century
3. R.L. TONGUE: *Somerset Folklore*, Folklore Society, 1965
4. J.G. FRAZER: *The Golden Bough*, Chapter xlviii, Macmillan, 1922

5. *Somerset and Dorset Notes and Queries*, Vol II, 1891. The Ooser described belonged to a Mr Cave of Hold Farm, Melbury Osmond; it has since been stolen
6. PENNETHORNE HUGHES: *Witchcraft*, Longmans, Green, 1954
7. Quoted by William Sandys: *Christmastide*, JOHN RUSSEL SMITH 1852
8. J. MARINGER: *The Gods of Prehistoric Man*, translated by Mary Ilford, Weidenfeld & Nicolson, 1956
9. H.R. ELLIS DAVIDSON: *Pagan Scandinavia*, Thames & Hudson, 1967
10. E. HASTED: *The History and Topographical Survey of the County of Kent*, Vol VI, 2nd edition, 1798
11. GEORGE WALDRON: *Description of the Isle of Man*, 1731
12. MRS H.A. BULLOCK: *History of the Isle of Man*, 1816
13. WILLIAM YARRELL *History of British Birds*, edited by Rev. A. Newton, Vol II Jan de Voorgt, 1843
14. RALPH WHITLOCK: *In Search of Lost Gods*, Phaidon, 1979
15. JOHN BIRTWHISTLE: Poem *St Stephen's Day*
16. GEORGE HENDERSON: *Folklore of the Northern Counties*, 1866

8 ♦ MUMMERS AND GUIZERS

At Chrissimass, at Chrissimass
Long time ago
Brave St George he singed aloud
All in the snow

Somerset Carol[1]

Ralph Whitlock claims that the hunting of the little troglodyte wren, with its fondness for rocks and caves, 'is a parallel to the Mumming plays, in which the champion of darkness is slain and the world brought back to life'.[2] That was the gist of all animal sacrifices, and of the supreme human sacrifice of which they were frequently a substitute. The point of the sacrifice was to ensure the fertility of the land; and it is with the land of England that the legendary figure of St George is identified. He was said to have been torn into ten parts and revived by the archangel Michael; and this theme of death and resurrection is central to all the mumming plays in which, in one form or another, he plays a central part.

This St George is a complex figure, known indiscriminately as saint or king (sometimes even as King William for William of Orange). The confusion indicates his main attributes, for he stands as both priest and monarch. In the first role he is the chief celebrant of the mid-winter sacrifice and in the second he stands for the land itself.

The drama that grew up around him, and which degenerated into the harmless annual farce of the mummers' plays, had its distant origin in the awful human sacrifices of mid-winter. At one time the priest, or divine king, who stood in place of the sun god to the people, was so closely identified with the annual course of the sun that he had to be killed at the solstice and replaced by a new king who would lead the people in the coming year. At best this ritual killing could be postponed for as long as the reigning king could prove his strength and potency.

As time went by the ritual was modified still further and a slave was appointed to stand as substitute for the king, becoming the victim in his place. Then, as we have already seen, in more recent centuries, animals took the place of these human sacrifices; but the idea that the fertility and fortunes of the land depended on the fate of the monarch at the solstice was not quickly forgotten.

The notion that it would be favourable for both king and country if a new reign started at mid-winter lay behind the Christmas Day coronations of William the Conqueror and Edmund, King and Martyr. The latter is particularly significant, for St Edmund was already linked to the sun when Humbert, Bishop of Elmham, crowned him at Bury St Edmunds in 855. When his father, the Saxon prince Alkmund, was on a pilgrimage to Rome, the sun shone with such brilliance on his breastplate as he prayed that a prophetess declared this to be a sign that his son would become justly great. The associations of Edward the Confessor as a winter king all came together in 1065, when the Anglo-Saxon chroniclers tell us that he 'came to Westminster towards Christmas and there had the abbey church consecrated which he himself had built to the glory of God, St Peter and all God's saints; the consecration of this church was on Holy Innocents' Day (28 December); and he passed away on the vigil of the Epiphany (6 January 1066) in the same abbey church.'[3] On the Christmas Day at the end of that year, the *Chronicle* relates, Archbishop Ealdred consecrated William of Normandy as King of England.

Even in historic times, kings have been killed as well as crowned at the winter solstice; and although their deaths did not take the public form of ritual sacrifice there are those who believe that they must be accounted for in that way. The fact that the Plantagenets were known to be closely involved with pre-Christian practices makes the choice of 6 January (Twelfth Day or Epiphany) for the murder of Richard II in 1400 particularly ominous. Another possible victim was Richard Plantagenet, illegitimate son of Richard III, who died at Eastwell in Kent on 22 December 1550.

The solstice killing which is of the greatest moment, however, happened over 400 years earlier. That was the murder of Thomas à Becket. He was born at the winter solstice (21 December) 1118 and murdered in Canterbury cathedral on 28 December, fifty-two years later. Many people believe that he deliberately chose to be a substitute for Henry II, by whose command he was killed; and that he was so well aware of the significance of his coming death that he actually arranged for the killing to take place on the cathedral steps at the time the solstice sun was setting.

It was solemn killings such as this that gave shape to the knock-about farce of the mummers' plays. They were performed by the villagers, partly as a way of collecting a bit of extra cash for the winter festivities; but more compulsively as a continuation of a tradition that it was unthinkable to break. The parts were taken by the same people year after year, and often handed down from father to son.

Everyone knew exactly what sort of entertainment they were in for. Just like our traditional Christmas pantomime, the Christmas mummers' plays, which for centuries flourished in southern and central England, followed a conventional pattern, despite several local variations. The performance always began with a presenter, who pleaded for:

'A room, a room, a garland room
I come to clear the way
And many follow after me
To show you sport and play'.

That piece of doggerel was spoken by a boy dressed up in girl's clothes at the beginning of the mummers' play at Sudbury near Harrow. Although the verse varied slightly from place to place the opening words always followed the same gist. They all indicate quite clearly that the play which is about to be performed is, like our pantomimes, an absolutely secular affair, with only rare and tenuous connections with those episodes in the medieval mystery plays that dramatise the Nativity.

The very simplicity of the doggerel verse also shows that the mummers' plays were based on oral tradition. Such texts as we possess were mostly written down in the nineteenth century. By that time they had incorporated matter belonging to the Napoleonic Wars and to other events and personages in British history that were far removed in place and time from the plays' origins in pagan ritual.

Mummers and Guizers ♦ 103

The main action of all the plays is the combat in which Saint or King George slays the forces of evil. That stage fight is loosely connected with the sword dances that evolved from the old fertility rites and which in many places – North Yorkshire being one recorded example – were performed up to the nineteenth century from St Stephen's Day to New Year.[4]

In the plays, George doesn't fight a dragon. Instead he takes on a human contestant, variously known as the Turkish Knight, the King of Egypt or simply as Slasher. Whoever the challenger is, he is usually the son of another character. The high point of the play is the mock combat between St George and his adversary, which is more notable for the opportunities it presents for the comic knockabout that delighted the audience than for any solemn reminder of ancient ritual.

The fight always ends with an odd twist. As you would expect, St George is invariably victorious, but the next part of the play concerns the revival of his dead opponent. This revival follows a lament for his death, often spoken by his father, who is sometimes known as the King of Egypt. In the play from Longborough in Gloucestershire there is a strong biblical echo in the father's lament. He cries:

> 'Horrible, terrible, what hast thou done?
> Thou has killed my only, dearly belov'd Son.'

Sometimes the lament is taken up by the other members of the cast, but in all cases it is speedily followed up by a call for the doctor who is to effect the cure. His entrance gives rise to the only bit of sustained dialogue in the play. It is deliberately comic. First there is a haggle over the fee, during which the doctor (who is sometimes played by Father Christmas) boasts of his skill at curing all sorts of diseases. The cure is always effective, and as the dead challenger revives he is greeted by such words as 'Rise up, bold fellow and fight again.'[5] Sometimes this injunction is taken literally and the audience have the fun of a second and sometimes even of a third fight.

The plays always ended with some more horseplay by a collection of diverse characters whose role was simply to entertain and collect money from the crowd. They sometimes had subsidiary fights of their own. At Odiham in Hampshire, for instance, Old Father Abraham is killed by his son Jack in a fight that symbolises the killing of the old year by the new, and the old man's death is described as being 'just like the setting sun'. In other places Jack represents a version of Everyman, burdened by his wife and numerous children whom he has to carry in effigy in a pack on his back. He is accompanied by Beelzebub, and by a fool, who is variously named. Sometimes Father Christmas, if he has not stood in for the doctor, takes a part with this throng. Some places found room for such characters as King Cole and King Alfred and his bride, and many of them included historical figures from recent times such as Nelson, Napoleon and General Wolfe. A version from Heptonstall in Yorkshire includes a Suffragette, while in Wing, Buckinghamshire, a local notable, Dr Dodd, the vicar who was hanged for forgery in 1777, makes an appearance.[6]

Apart from Father Christmas, the two main legendary characters to appear in the plays are Robin Hood and Little John. Although they have crept in from the midsummer and May Day revels of which they are more legitimately a part, it is fitting that they should appear in a play that re-enacts the old rites of the renewal of vegetation, for Robin Hood is the essential Green Man.

Certainly the costumes that the mummers wore were meant to remind the audience that the players represented natural forces. Often they wore cloaks covered in torn strips of paper which stood for leaves and feathers. In addition each character wore some peculiarly distinguishing feature. The Abingdon mummers of Oxfordshire gave their Old Slasher (sometimes known as Bean Slasher or Bear Slasher) a green paper hat; while St George wore a crown, carried a sword and had blue decorations on his paper coat. At the beginning of the nineteenth century, John Latham of Romsey reported that the mummers 'dress themselves in a Manner in which the Shirt is ever uppermost decorated with Ribbons of various Colours tied about their arms, waist and legs.'[7]

The mummers' plays were regularly performed in many villages until the early years of this century, and in several places they have recently been revived. The archaeologist O.G.S. Crawford recalls seeing the mummers perform their little play in the family kitchen when he was a boy at East Woodhay. 'The plot was simple and consisted chiefly in a duel between "old King Jarge" and a "Turkish Knight", in which both in turn are killed, and then brought to life again by a doctor. The mummers were entirely covered face and all by a garb of ribbons.'⁸ In 1910, Ditchfield reported, 'We still have our Berkshire mummers at Christmas, who come to us disguised in strange garb.'⁹ The hero of that Berkshire play introduced himself in rhyming couplets:

> 'I am King George, that noble champion bold
> And with my trusty sword I won ten thousand pounds in gold:
> 'Twas then I fought the fiery dragon, and brought him to the slaughter,
> And by these means I won the King of Egypt's daughter.'

A Somerset gardener from the Quantocks had a more confused memory of the mummers' play that took place in Storgussey before the First World War, when he was a boy. 'They had black faces,' he recalled in 1956, 'and they had a banjo and concertina and the bones, and they danced in the village. Yes, there was King George and Father Christmas and one of them dies and I remember they sang "This poor old soul is dead".'¹⁰

Later west country revivals of the mummers' plays are still performed at Marshfield near Chippenham and at Keynsham just outside Bristol. They offer a striking contrast. The seven Marshfield mummers wear the traditional torn paper shirts over their Sunday best suits, and the parts are played by the same people year after year. Each Boxing Day the play is performed five times at different places along the village high street. The text that is used was put together by the vicar's sister in 1930, after her brother had heard the vicarage gardener reciting lines that he said came from the old village play. The tradition of an annual performance by the mummers was revived in 1931 and has been kept up since then.

The Keynsham mummers work from a text written down in 1822, which they have performed every Boxing Day for the last five years. Their play is an altogether more sophisticated affair, with the cast dressed up according to a more modern idea of theatrical costume. With their board inscribed 'Clap Now', which they hold up at the end of each performance through the town, they are a long way from the crude and sometimes violent begging of the early mummers. For because the plays were partly a means of getting beer money for the actors, rival casts sometimes found themselves engaged in real fights over the tributes to their mock combats.

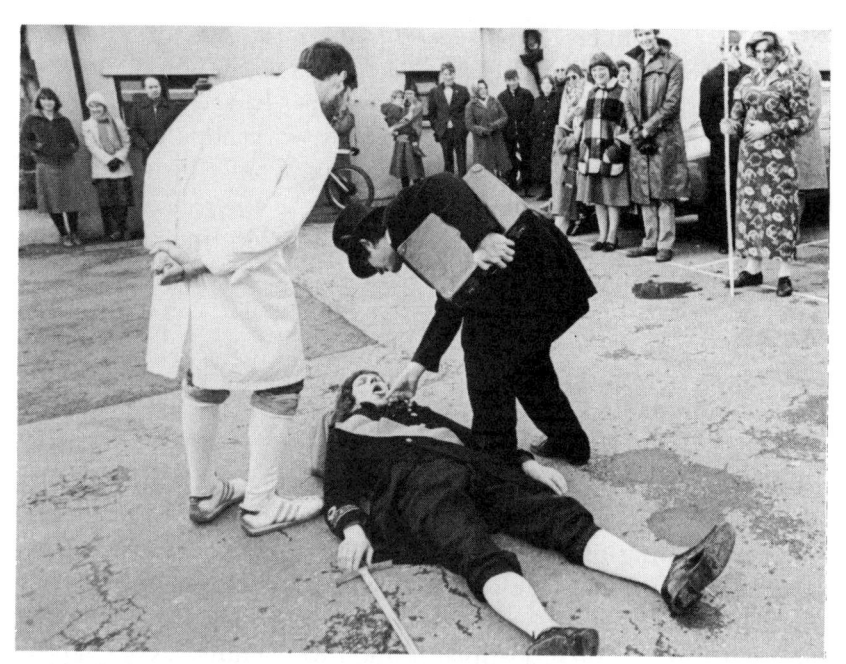

Bold Slasher brought back to life at Keynsham

and at Marshfield

Mummers and Guizers ♦ 107

On 23 December 1865, *The Wiltshire Times*[11] reported such a fight between the villagers of Melksham and South Wraxhall, when the 'youths of the plebian class' as the paper had it, arrayed in the 'ragged remnants of some paperhanger's workshop', congregated at the Unicorn public house in Melksham, from which they were speedily evicted. The fight continued to the town bridge, which was 'quickly strewn, not with corpses, but with the remnants of Wraxhall paperhangings'. In many places such Christmas fights were a more organised part of the mid-winter ceremonies. At Bridgnorth in Shropshire it was traditional for small boys with blackened faces to hold single stick combats every Boxing Day.

Ironically it is customs such as that, and the debased and chaotic activities of some nineteenth-century mummers, far more than sophisticated revivals like the one at Keynsham, that take us back to the ancient origins of these plays in the priestly rites connected with the ritual killing of the divine king.

From Palaeolithic cave paintings we know that these rites were performed by men dressed as animals or birds. The medieval villagers who dressed up in a similar fashion were known as 'guizers' (a corruption of disguisers). They wore masks like the bull's head of the Dorset Ooser, or carried emblems to represent horses like the Kent hodening horse, both of which were mentioned in Chapter 7. These and other elaborate and often outrageous costumes were carefully preserved from year to year. In some way or another all of them were derived from the ritual garments worn by the medicine men or shamans who once conducted the sacrifices designed to propitiate the ancient horned god of vegetation. In historic times the remnant of that ritual was a noisy procession through the streets.

Long before the mummers' plays were performed, masked men such as these danced through and round the tribal village enclosure at mid-winter. It was on their exact and meticulous performance of each detail of the ritual that the renewal of the sun and the fortunes of the next season's harvest were thought to depend. So the men who took part in the ceremonies were the greatest in the land. When the Christian Church became established these persistent pagan practices were frowned upon, and the high-ranking wearers of the animal masks and skins were replaced by the poorest people in the village, who often used a tradition of whose origins they were only dimly aware as an excuse for begging. The strength of the tradition can be measured by the way it survived the edict of Archbishop Theodore, who in 690 prescribed penances 'for anyone who on the Kalends of January clothe themselves in the skins of cattle and carry heads of animals.'

Like all winter rituals, those of the guizers start in November; and our tradition of turnip masks at Hallowe'en is one last reminder of the masked dances at Samhain. Indeed a description of the customs in Scotland throughout the eighteenth and nineteenth centuries reads like an elaborate and sinister version of our Hallowe'en parties. For there the men wore masks or blackened their faces to impersonate the dead, or to hide from them in various fantastic shapes. The disguise was also useful as a means of safeguarding them from the vengeance of the living on whom they played pranks (reminiscent of the trick-or-treat games that have recently returned to this country from America) such as blocking chimneys with turf in order to deflect the smoke.[12] At Hallowmass in Shetland the guizers were more directly linked to the corn spirit than to the dead or mischievous demons. The youths who begged from house to house there were known as sheklers and they wore straw dresses.

In Cheshire, with its custom of eating soul cakes at Hallowe'en (*see* Chapter 2) the mummers or guizers were known as 'soulers'. By the nineteenth century their grotesque antics were accepted by the gentry as a venerable country custom. Writing in her diary for 1871, Margaret Leicester Warren of Old Hall, Tabley[13] recalled that on 'All Souls' Eve after dinner we were told that the soulers were in the hall. We went down as we had never seen them before and here was found 4 or 5 men one of whom was dressed up as a horse, his legs serving for the hind legs of the animal and a stick for the poor creature's third leg. He had enormous jaws which he continually clapped together and huge bead eyes. The men sang a song about "apples and strong beer" hoping Papa would go down to his cellar and see what he could find as they wouldn't come a-souling for another year and so on. The horse made sundry jumps and kicks and the entertainment was concluded.'

In more recent times, and with full civic blessing, the elaborate North Somerset pageants, which draw vast sums of money for local charities during the first half of November, carry out the tradition of the Hallowe'en guizers.

The next season at which the guizers appear is at Christmas itself, and here it is often quite difficult to distinguish their processions from debased forms of the mummers' plays. A Somerset carter, Ted Hunt, who took part in the traditional Christmas revelries at the turn of this century described what happened.[14] There were five of them, he remembered, 'all dressed up in all sorts. There was one dressed up as an old 'ooman and she did give your back-side a good bang with a stick at times. Yes, we did black our faces and we went all round Bicknoller and Stogumber and Lydeard St Lawrence different nights.'

In West Cornwall, where the guizers were known as goose or geese dancers, the parades through the streets went on from Christmas to Twelfth Night. The participants wore the traditional bull masks and carried the wooden horse's head with the device to make the creature open and shut his mouth. The processions became so rowdy that in 1870 the corporation of Penzance tried to put an end to the custom. Notices were posted in conspicuous places forbidding the Geesedancers to appear in the streets; but bureaucracy proved ineffective against the ancient tradition, and when W.H. Hudson visited the area in the early years of this century he found it still flourishing. At St Ives, he discovered that, 'night after night, a considerable part of the inhabitants turn out in masks and any fantastic costume they can manufacture . . . and dance on the beach to some simple music till 11 o'clock or later . . . This goes on for a fortnight. And they are Methodists, good, sober people.'[15]

From an eighteenth century observer we have a report of how the New Year was celebrated by the guizers in Scotland during the eighteenth century. He described how 'one of the company dressed himself in a cow's hide, upon which the rest of the party belaboured him with sticks. They all then left the house, and ran around it, only being readmitted on repeating the following words, which are still preserved in St Kilda: "May God bless this house and all that belongs to it, cattle, stones and timber. In plenty of meat, of bed and body clothes, and health of men may it ever abound." Each then pulled off a piece of the hide and burnt it for the purpose of driving away demons.'

Usually, however, the guizers, unlike the mummers (whose name suggests that they too originally mimed their plays), had no formal words to say. There must have been a lot of impromptu backchat though, and most of it much less lyrical than anything once heard on the now uninhabited St Kilda, as the guizers went round with their begging bowls. For the processions seem to have become increasingly rowdy with the centuries.

If the guizers did not continue their festivities throughout the whole twelve days of Christmas as they did in Cornwall, they came out again on Twelfth Night itself, and once again a horse, or its emblem, was the central feature. On the Isle of Man 'the laare vane' or white mare was traditionally brought in to the Twelfth Night supper. This creature was made up out of a wooden horse's head with a snapping mouth controlled by a man concealed under a white sheet.

Other Twelfth Night rituals are more perplexing. Nobody knows for certain what the Haxey Hood game in Lincolnshire is supposed to celebrate, but its origin is certainly very ancient. The number of people officially taking part represent the thirteen members of a witches' coven. They include a fool, a lord and eleven 'bogies', a name which Margaret Murray[16] believes to be derived from a debased word for the old pagan gods. Once the game is under way, spectators are able to join in and take part in a sort of rugger in which the hoods have to be pushed or kicked into a set of prearranged goals. The last one – the Haxey Hood itself – is aimed at the inn.

A much more domestic but equally ancient Twelfth Night game concerned the crowning of the bean king, who had to be chosen by lot. The bean was hidden in a cake, in much the same way as trinkets are hidden in the Christmas pudding, and whoever took the piece that held the bean was king for the subsequent merrymaking. The only snag was that he had to pay for the drinks, a reminder of his original role as the sacrificial victim (*see* Chapter 2). The Twelfth Night king might hold his court among the highest in the land; for these were courtly festivities unlike the revels of the mummers and guizers in the villages. Shakespeare was only one of the Elizabethan and Jacobean poets who was commissioned to write plays to be performed on such occasions.

The last appearance of the winter guizers was on Plough Monday, at the end of the holiday. Up to the middle of the last century, the Oxfordshire ploughboys dressed up in fantastic costumes and paraded the plough through the village, shouting:

'Rain, Hail or Shine
The best cock in the yard's mine,'

In Somerset, Plough Monday was quite openly used as an excuse for begging. The farm labourers drew a plough decorated with ribbons through the village streets and anyone foolish enough not to contribute to the begging bowl could expect to have his lawn ploughed up. Up to the time of the Reformation, a fool, representing Pan, the devil or the Green Man, capered behind the plough dressed in animal skins to which a tail was attached. The Cambridgeshire Plough Monday beggars had an equally fantastic central character. This was the straw bear,[17] a man completely covered in straw, whose costume clearly indicated his connection with the coming harvests.

Although the Plough Monday celebrations were obvious remnants of pagan ceremonial, the Church on the whole seems to have tolerated them. In Hull the miracle play of Noah was performed on Plough Monday in Holy Trinity church throughout the fifteenth century, and in many places up to the Reformation a light, known as 'the plough light', burnt in the churches at this time (see Chapter 6). Even now at this season ploughs are blessed in the naves of some village churches. These serious tokens of man's ultimate dependence on his co-operation with nature underlie even the most bawdy of the antics devised by the mummers and guizers; although the sterner nonconformists did not always see it that way. At the end of the last century, W. Antliff, D.D. wrote to his local paper to say 'When the Primitive Methodists missioned the county of Leicester . . . There prevailed among other practices, a system of going round the country on what is called Plough Monday, and in the most fantastic and ridiculous costumes, performing the most foolish and absurd exhibitions. The money collected during the day by this system was carried at night to the public house where scenes of revelry and devilry were enacted that often terminated most disastrously. The men who had recourse to this vile system were in that part distinguished by the name of "plough-bullocks".'[18]

Generally, however, as the ceremonies of the Church took over many of the pagan rituals of the farming year, the two strands became inextricably confused. The Somerset gypsy mummers had a song for New Year's Day that referred both to the Christian legends of Joseph of Arimathea's visit to that county and to the local industries of mining and farming:

> Here come Three Josephs, Three Josephs are here,
> All for to bring 'ee the Luck of the Year.
> One he did stand at the Babe's right hand,
> One was a Lord in Egypt's land,
> One was a tinner and sailed the sea,
> God keep you merry, say we.
> God bless the cattle, the corn and hay,
> And the skill of your timber and tools alway.
> And God send the workers good metal and fire.[19]

The most astounding marriage of pagan and Christian rites took place during the reign of Mary Tudor, at the feast of the conversion of St Paul, which is celebrated on 25 January. On that day an extraordinary procession went through the streets of London to the cathedral, bringing a live buck and doe to the high altar. It has been suggested that this was done to commemorate the fact that a temple of Diana formerly stood on the site; but the ritual cannot be unconnected with the observances to the horned god, Cernunnos.

That god is honoured much more boisterously in the horn dance

Abbots Bromley Horn Dance, Staffordshire

Mummers and Guizers ♦ 113

at Abbots Bromley in Staffordshire, now performed on the first Sunday after 4 September, but originally forming part of the Christmas and Twelfth Night festivities of the village. The six participants still carry wooden reindeer heads with real horns attached to them. Three of the heads are painted white, three are black, and the point of the game is a mock combat between the forces of light and darkness. Ralph Whitlock[20] sees the whole occasion as a 'simulated deer hunt', and believes that it may have its origin in rites of sympathetic magic practised by Neolithic hunters.

Even if that is so, the fact that the ritual has become so established suggests that it was an important fertility rite long after men had ceased to depend on hunting as a main source of food. The Celts must have interpreted it as a rite of Cernunnos, the nature god whose observances were vital to the renewal of the earth after the barren winter. Primitive man felt responsible for ordering the course of nature, and never took the seasons for granted for he knew that his survival depended on close attention to the rhythm of the year, and all the winter solstice customs that have been handed down to us neglect that need.

References:
1. R.L. TONGUE: *Somerset Folklore*, Folklore Society, 1965
2. RALPH WHITLOCK: *In Search of Lost Gods*, Phaidon, 1979
3. *Anglo Saxon Chronicle*, Parter MS, translated by G.N. Garmonsway, Everyman, Dent, 1953
4. *Gentleman's Magazine*, May 1811
5. Elaboration of the Gloucestershire, Weston-sub-Edge play, given by E.K. CHAMBERS in *The English Folk Play*, 1933; Reprinted: Oxford, 1969
6. H.W. HARWOOD and F.H. MARSDEN: Introductory study to the Midgley Version of *The Pace Egg*, Halifax, 1935
7. JOHN LATHAM: Collection for a history of Romsey, Hampshire, quoted by G.C. Cawte, Alex Helm and N. Peacock in *English Ritual Drama*, Folklore Society, 1967
8. O.G.S. CRAWFORD: *The Eye Goddess*, Phoenix House, 1957
9. PETER HAMPSON DITCHFIELD: *Vanishing England*, Methuen, 1910
10. R.L. TONGUE: *Somerset Folklore*, Folklore Society, 1965
11. Reported in *Roomer*, Vol I, i, September 1980

12. F. MARION MCNEIL: *Hallowe'en*, Albyn Press, 1970
13. Researched by Joan Leach
14. R.L. TONGUE: *Somerset Folklore*, Folklore Society, 1965
15. W.H. HUDSON: *The Land's End*, Hutchinson, 1908
16. MARGARET A. MURRAY: *The God of the Witches*, Sampson Low, Marston & Co., 1931
17. ENID PORTER: *Cambridgeshire Customs*, Routledge & Kegan Paul, 1969
18. IDWAL JONES: Report in *Roomer*, Vol I, ii, December 1980
19. Collected by RUTH TONGUE: quoted by Christina Hole: *Saints in Folklore*, Bell, 1966
20. RALPH WHITLOCK: *In Search of Lost Gods*, Phaidon, 1979

THE WINTER FESTIVALS

31 October	St Bartholomew's Fair	25 December	Birth of Christ (Christmas Day)
	Hallow E'en	26 December	Boxing Day
			St Stephen's Day
1 November	All Saints' Day		The Hunting of the Wren
	New Year, Isle of Man until eighteenth century	31 December	Hogmanay
	Samhain	1 January	Roman feast of the Kalends of January
2 November	All Souls' Day		New Year
5 November	Guy Fawkes' Day	5 January	Old Christmas Day
11 November	St Martin's Day	6 January	Twelfth Night
	Teutonic New Year		Epiphany
	Armistice Day		The following Monday is kept as Plough Monday
15 November	Roman feast of Jupiter		
22 November	St Cecilia's Day		
23 November	St Clement's Day	11 January	Old New Year
25 November	St Catherine's Day	13 January	Sunrise alignment, Swinside Circle, Millom, Cumbria
30 November	St Andrew's Day		
		17 January	Old Twelfth Night
13 December	St Lucia's Day, Swedish Festival of Light	21 January	St Agnes' Day
		25 January	Feast of the Conversion of St Paul
17 December	Start of the Roman Saturnalia (lasting 7 days)	29 January	Up Helly Aa, Shetland
19 December	Start of two-day festival of Opalia, in honour of Ops, wife of Saturn	1 February	Imbolc
		2 February	Candlemas
		3 February	Feast of St Blaize
21 December	Winter Solstice Thomasmas (Day of St Thomas the apostle) Birth of Mithras, Apollo, Dionysius, Odin and the Phrygian God Attis		

116 ♦ The Winter Solstice

INDEX

Abbots Bromley 113, 114
Abingdon 105
Aconite 83, 84
Adonis 34, 50, 80
Advent 64, 89
Ahriman 34, 35
All Hallows 5, 55–57, 84
All Hallows Eve 25, 26
All Saints 3, 27, 50
All Souls 27, 51, 57, 62, 84
Anglesey 90
Anglo-Saxon Chronicle 51
Ann 24
Antliff, W. 112
Aphrodite 34
Apollo 8, 35, 77
Apple 73, 74
Archangel Michael 101
Archbishop Theodore 109
Arizona 14, 15
Armistice Day 27, 60
Ashen Faggot 66
Attis 34
Aubrey, John 2, 37, 48
Avalon 73, 80
Avebury 14, 16, 25

Balder the Beautiful 50
Barley 70
Barnatt, John 10
Bath 41
Bayes 74, 75
Beans 72, 111
Bede 39, 45, 51
Beelzebub 105
Ben Nevis 28
Benty Grange 48
Beowulf 45, 48
Bera 28
Bestla 46
Bishop Martin of Bracea 74
Bishopsgate 55
Black Godiva 89
Blacksmiths 61
Blotmonath or Bloodmonth 45, 88
Boar 48, 49, 95
Boke of Curtasye 55
Bonfire 58, 59, 61
Bor 46

Box (plant) 85
Boxing Day 106, 108
Boyne, River 7, 90
Brand, John 87
Bridestones Long Barrow 29
Brigantia 40
Brigit, Bride, Briid 23, 24, 28
Brown, George Mackay 52, 65
Brumalia 33
Buckinghamshire 81, 84, 105
Bull 34, 90
Bury St. Edmunds 43, 102

Caesar 20, 23, 35, 38
Cambridgeshire 112
Candlemas 3, 5, 28, 45, 56, 68, 69, 83, 85
Canterbury 1, 38–40
Canterbury cathedral 103
Canute 50
Capricorn 37
Carn Euny 11–12
Castlerigg 28, 69
Cattle 25, 87, 89
Cautes 35
Cautopates 35
Cave Gate 35, 83
Celts 3, 5, 17, 18–31, 33, 35–36, 40, 44, 49–50, 56, 72–73, 79, 114
Cerdic 51
Ceres 68
Ceridwen 30
Cerne Abbas 23–24
Cernunnos 19, 24, 113–114
Chaco Canyon 15
Chatham 61
Cheshire 26, 109
Chi-ro 40
Christ 2, 23, 30, 40, 43, 48, 49, 50, 68, 76, 87, 88, 89
Christianity 32, 38
Christians 1, 2, 37–38, 39, 40–41, 45, 52, 113
Christingle 63–64
Christmas 1, 2, 40, 48, 51, 53, 55, 64, 71, 74–75, 79–80, 94, 97, 99, 110, 111, 114
Christmas Day 5, 44, 81, 87, 102
Christmas Eve 1, 66, 75–76, 78, 82, 87, 91
Christmas Pantomime 103
Christmas Pudding 33, 111

Index ◆ 117

Christmas Rose 80
Christmas Tree 79–80
Chrysostom 2
Church of England Children's Society 62
Colorado 15
Compitalia 41, 84
Connemarra 99
Constantine, emperor 38
Corn dolly 71, 91
Cornwall 11–12, 16, 66, 73, 87, 98, 110–111
Coventry 89
Crawford, O.G.S. 90, 105
Crete 8, 89
Cromwell 82
Cumbria 10–11, 23, 28, 48, 69
Cybele 34

Dagda 23, 28
Danelaw 44
Danes 46, 48, 50, 94
Dartmoor 7, 10, 14, 46, 65
Davidson, Hilda 45, 46, 94
Denmark 24
Derbyshire 10, 49, 57
Devon 59, 66
Diana 113
Diocletian 37, 62
Dionysius 35, 91
Dorchester-on-Thames 14
Dorset 19, 22, 23
Dorset Cursus 11, 13–14, 16, 18
Dorset Ooser 89–90, 108
Druids 2, 14, 18, 20–21, 30, 32, 35, 38, 56, 78–79, 83, 98
Dublin 47

Earconbert, King 50
Easter 1, 51, 85
Eliot, T.S. 30, 37
Epiphany 64, 67–68, 95, 102
Epona or Esus 24, 37
Erasmus 79
Essex 85
Europa 90
Evergreens 74–77
Everyman 105
Exmoor 22
Exmoor pony 93
Eyam Moor 10

Fairies 16, 26, 73
Fairless, Michael 2
Father Christmas 15, 47, 104–106
Februa 40, 68
Fiorgynn 49
Fogous 11–12, 15
Frazer, J.G. 56, 88, 91, 94
Freyja 48
Freyr 48–49, 93

Frigg 49–50
Frilford 22–23

Gardiner, Gerald B. 9
Gay, John 75
General Woolfe 105
Germany 79
Gildas 50
Gilgamesh 90
Glastonbury 38
Glastonbury Thorn 80–82
Glastonbury Tor 21
Gloucestershire 23, 38, 67, 104
Glover, John 10, 69
Gonds 46
Gordon, Ruth St Leger 16
Gosfirth Cross 48
Grail 30
Graves, Robert 90
Great Mother 9, 34, 36, 66, 90
Green Children of Woolpit 72
Green Knight 30–31, 75
Green Man 105, 112
Gregorian Calendar 5
Grimes Graves 47
Grimm, Brothers 52, 98
Guizers 108–111
Guy Fawkes 26, 57–59, 72

Häggeby Stone 93–94
Hallowe'en 57, 67, 73, 109
Hampshire 61, 104
Hanukkah 62, 64–65
Harding, D.W. 22
Hardy, Thomas 87, 88
Hatherleigh 59
Hawkes, Jacquetta 4
Haxey Hood 111
Hazelnuts 27, 72–73
Helya's Night 52
Herbert, George 69
Herefordshire 19, 82, 87
Hertfordshire 35, 83
Hill of Tara 23, 56
Hindu Festival of Lights 62
Hob 30
Hogmanay 67, 99
Holly 75–76
Holy Innocents' Day 102
Hook Norton 37
Horse 93–94
Housesteads 35
Hudson, W.H. 110
Hughes, Ted 70
Hunt, Ted 110

Iceland 45
Imbolc 3, 5, 20, 27–28, 31, 38, 40, 45, 61, 68

118 ♦ **The Winter Solstice**

Ireland 7–8, 18, 24, 56, 72
Isis 34
Isle of Man 26, 28, 56, 67, 82, 87, 95–96
Isle of Skye 73
Ivy 75–77

Jefferies, Richard 4, 80
Josephus 64
Julian the Apostate 38
Juniper 77–78
Jupiter 39–40

Kalends of January 5, 66, 109
Kent 95
Kent hodening horse 92–93, 108
Keynsham 106–108
Kilvert, Francis 81, 87
King Alfred 25, 40, 44, 105
King Arthur 30, 75
King Charles 1, 82
King Cole 105
King Edward the Confessor 102
King Ethelred 68
King George 104, 106
King Henry 11, 103
King of Egypt 104
King Richard 11, 102
King William of Orange 101
King William the Conqueror 102
Kipling, Rudyard 32
Kivas 14–15, 47, 56
Knutsford 26

Laare Vane 111
Lady Day 56
Lancashire 57
Land's End 28
Lapland 47
Latham, John 105
Lawrence, D.H. 7
Leicestershire 22
Lewes 58
Lincolnshire 22, 83, 111
Little John 105
Littlecote Park 39
Lochgilphead 10
Lockyer, Sir Norman 28
Loki 50
London 113
Longborough 104
Long Meg 10–11
Lucifer 30
Lupercalia 40
Luther, Martin 79
Lydney 23, 38

Maiden Castle 22–23, 38
Maponus or Mabon 35
Mars 24, 40, 68

Marshfield 106–107
Martinmas 39, 56, 60–61, 68
Mary Tudor 113
Maundy Thursday 55
Maximus 39
May Day 3, 85, 105
Mediterranean 4, 37
Mercury 47
Mexico 4
Midsummer Night's Dream 16
Minerva 40
Mistletoe 21, 78, 98
Mithras 32, 34–36, 38, 47, 89, 99
Moravia 62, 64
Moray Firth 67
Mother Night 51
Mother's Cap 10
Mummers 16, 67, 103, 106, 101–110, 112
Murray, Margaret 14, 16, 111

Nativity 103
Nerthus 47, 49
New Mexico 14, 15
New Year 5, 6, 25, 33, 56, 60, 66, 67, 76, 82, 84, 93, 95, 98, 99, 110, 112
Newgrange 7–10, 13, 15, 26
Nidhogg 48
Niffheim 48
Noah 112
Nodens 23, 38
Norfolk 34
North American Indians 14–16, 56
Northumberland 34, 67
Norway 45

Odin 24, 43–44, 46–47, 49–50, 51, 72, 79, 91, 93
Olaf the Holy 45
Old Bronzen Face 89
Old Christmas 5, 81, 82
Ops 33
Orkney 7, 52, 65–66
Orpheus 39
Osiris 34, 90
Ovid 32
Oxfordshire 105, 111

Pan 112
Paps of Jura 11
Peterborough 46
Pliny 21, 35
Plough Monday 41, 84–85, 111–112
Pope Gregory 50
Pope Zacharius 66
Procopius 44
Puck 30
Puritans 1, 2, 75

Quetzalcoatl 4

Index ♦ 119

Ragnorak 48
Ribchester 35
Romans 31, 32–42, 62, 72, 74, 80
Rome 33, 35, 38, 102
Rosemary 74–77
Ross, Anne 20, 30, 36

Sagittarius 37
Sambain 3, 5, 20, 25–28, 31, 38, 39, 51, 56–59, 61, 72, 88, 109
Santa Claus 47
Saturnalia 31, 33, 36, 40, 44, 62, 77
Saxons 42, 44, 45, 50
Scandinavia 4, 44, 45
Schrimir 48
Scorpio 37
Scotland 10, 28, 57, 72, 77, 91, 109, 110
Shakespeare 16, 111
Shaman 15, 47
Sheffield 10, 49
Shetland 52–53, 109
Siberia 47
Sipapu 15
Sir Gawain 30–31, 75
Sir Gawain and the Green Knight 30
Slasher 104–105, 107
Sleipnir 46–47, 50, 91
Smith, Sydney 94
Snowdrop 83
Somerset 60, 66, 73, 81, 88, 106, 109, 110
Soulers 109
St Agnes 37, 80
St Augustine 2, 39
St Bartholomew 56
St Bridget 28, 40, 61, 68
St Catherine 76, 84
St Clement 61
St Columba 18
St Edmund 102
St Francis 88
St Joseph 66
St Joseph of Arimathea 80, 113
St Martin 39, 60–62
St Mascen 39
St Patrick 62
St Paul's cathedral 113
St Peter 102
St Stephen 94, 95, 98, 104
St Thomas 52, 72, 75
Staffordshire 29, 71, 113–114
Stellmoor 91
Stephen the Evangelist 94
Stonehenge 8–10
Strabo 18
Straw Bear 112
Strenia 33
Stukeley, William 78
Sul-Minerva 41

Sussex 58, 95
Sutton Hoo 48–49
Swinside 10

Taleisin 30
Tarinus 24
Tarvos 89
Taylor, Rogan 47
Teutates 24
The Golden Bough 56
The Waste Land 30
Thomas à Becket 102
Thor 47–48, 66, 78
Three Kings 68
Tindles 57
Tongue, R.L. 88
Torah 64
Tul'ya's E'en 52
Turkish Knight 104–105
Turner, William 1
Tusser, Thomas 94
Tutanes 19
Twelfth Night 5, 41, 56, 67–68, 73, 75, 76, 84, 110, 111, 114

Ulster 30
Up Helly Aa 53, 55

Venus 49
Vikings 44, 47
Virgin Mary 23, 28, 52, 68, 83

Wales 72, 83
Wayland Smith 62
Welsh *mari-lwyd* 93
West Stow 43
Weston, Jessie 30
Wheat 68, 71
Whiteleaved Oak 19, 21
Whitlock, Ralph 98, 101, 114
Wild Hunt 46
Wiltshire Christmas Bull 89
Wiltshire Times 108
Windmill Hill 25
Witches 14, 16, 57, 66, 76, 84, 89, 111
Woden 44, 46
Worcestershire 67
Wren 95–99
Wyoming 14, 16

Yggdrasil 48
Yorkshire 44, 71, 105
Yule 44–46, 48, 52, 66, 67, 91, 95
Yule Log 62, 66, 68

Zeus 90
Zodiac 37